PEACE
IN
PIECES

AN EXPERIENTIAL
DISCOURSE TO
SERENITY AND BALANCE

DR. M.K.R. KHAN

BALBOA.
PRESS
A DIVISION OF HAY HOUSE

Balboa Press books may be ordered through booksellers or by contacting:

Balboa Press
A Division of Hay House
1663 Liberty Drive
Bloomington, IN 47403
www.balboapress.com
1 (877) 407-4847

Because of the dynamic nature of the Internet, any web addresses or links contained in this book may have changed since publication and may no longer be valid. The views expressed in this work are solely those of the author and do not necessarily reflect the views of the publisher, and the publisher hereby disclaims any responsibility for them.

The author of this book does not dispense medical advice or prescribe the use of any technique as a form of treatment for physical, emotional, or medical problems without the advice of a physician, either directly or indirectly. The intent of the author is only to offer information of a general nature to help you in your quest for emotional and spiritual well-being. In the event you use any of the information in this book for yourself, which is your constitutional right, the author and the publisher assume no responsibility for your actions.

Any people depicted in stock imagery provided by Thinkstock are models, and such images are being used for illustrative purposes only. Certain stock imagery © Thinkstock.

Print information available on the last page.

ISBN: 978-1-5043-8058-4 (sc)
ISBN: 978-1-5043-8059-1 (hc)
ISBN: 978-1-5043-8064-5 (e)

Library of Congress Control Number: 2017907585

Balboa Press rev. date: 11/07/2017

In happy times praise God

In difficult times seek help of God

In quiet times worship God

In adverse times trust God

And at all other times thank God

In the name of God, the most gracious, the most merciful

I dedicate this book to ALLAH the only God, who is the Merciful, the Knower, the Protector, the Provider, the Sustainer and Omniscient Creator of this universe and pray for blessings and guidance from that supreme almighty.

I am obliged by the virtues of my religion, to ask for the forgiveness it warrants and pardon it seeks for any un-intentional or un-willing oversights committed in writing this book.

Suggestions and conclusions are invited from believers of any philosophy to extend any convincing answer or any understandable explanation, contrary to this book.

Author

Raaz

This book which is the first ever I have attempted to write, elicits appreciation and gratefulness towards God for enabling me to successfully bring it forth to all the readers. I thank my family for being so patient in attending to me with their intangible, subdued and unending help all along my work. I want to thank the team of RAAZ INC. 2317, W. Devon Ave., Chicago for sponsoring their care, assistance and expertise in letting this effort shape up into a draft and lastly I thank Dr. Shahid Ekbal for his support, encouragement and guidance without which this book could not have been completed.

Dr. M. K. R. Khan

DISCLAIMER

Study of Islamic literature is a universe in itself and I humbly admit that I am a student of my medical faculty only, not an Islamic scholar, nor have I done extensive research in this subject literally. I intend that this book may be considered as a voice of a common man holding decades of exposure to peaceful life, carrying virtues of a modest Muslim, following Islamic faith by birth and choice, and now trying to project a true value of a satisfying lifestyle and earnestly extending arms towards all, especially those who are unaware, incompletely aware or incorrectly aware of Islam, leading to ISLAM getting shattered into pieces.

This book by no means intends to be considered a contribution to literature but it is only a piece of practical and logical aspect of ISLAM, that I have lived by and understood as a commoner. Spread in few parts, it is not a translation of QORAN neither it is influenced by any sect, creed or any one school of thought .It presents only certain directives deduced after years of reading QORAN for self-education, referencing various translations written in my native language URDU, penning down my inferences and interpretations in my own words of English.

I do not dare proclaim that this book is complete or is a perfect reflection of Islamic ideology except that it is my chosen subject matter of text and comprehension considered relevant for readers in an attempt to familiarize with simple but necessary facts. But if the reader wishes to explore more of what is mentioned in this book or about ISLAM, QORAN and Prophet MOHAMED's biography and quotes, then there is treasure of knowledge with bibliographic references, historical research and celebrated data in Islamic journalism that can be obtained from Muslim scholars, Islamic foundations and mythical books.

Author

CONTENTS

PART I

UNDERSTANDING ISLAM

CHAPTER 1

We always wondered how the origin and existence of universe can be explained. Does it exist just because it is existing or this continued existence is a planned attempt with an organized system of galaxy along with its ecological balances provided for comfortable living of animal kingdom by some extraneous power and control? Is the universe existing for the survival of its inmates within and for a purpose or we are surviving on occurrence of some consequence of chance factors? Our inability to comprehend an answer for the same interprets the limitation of human intellect but the only plausible understanding seems to be the belief in control of some supernatural power.

Since times immemorial quoted sayings and documented quotations have presented deficient philosophy and unconvincing ideology, understandable to the existing psychology of human brain about this enquiry. The science of evolution was equally unsatisfactory to have contended the human mind of any given clarification. The history of mankind with its advent of scientific basis is giving only hypothetical explanations for theory of evolution, which remains unclear to the understanding of the human mind even till this date.

The concept of molecular biology of the living and the nuclear physics of the non-living is still underway with its research yet fails to educate us of any understanding of the etiology and the existence of the universe. Human beings though being a part of this universe are not led by default to understand the provisions of the provider and designation of the sustainer. The creation and sustenance of universe with its inhabitants, both living and non-living is itself beyond human capacity of understanding and introspection. Then comes the purpose of its creation and sustenance which also cannot be fully analyzed, unless there is acceptance of this mystery as God given, otherwise it will remain unresolved to the mankind forever.

The coexistence of animal kingdom with diverse species and human beings with innumerable castes and creeds divided by various religions and sects, the continuity of the human race by balance of births and deaths, the loss and survival through natural calamities, mysterious happenings and non-understandable mishaps all reflect a patronage of one great controller of this universe. Only sensible thinkers are elucidated to judge and admit that there must be some active force, some effective power and some supreme authority which is controlling this system of universe so well.

Time and again we have failed to grasp the truth that there is not much we or scientific inventions could have done for creation or survival of life in universe except the fact that, the happenings which are un-anticipated, the events which come un-expected and the outcomes which are unpredictable, only in the end make us believe that we do not know everything about our life and its environment. We do not understand the truth of our existence and human intelligence cannot encompass the knowledge other than what is revealed to them by science.

So the question remains as to who is responsible for this harmonious balance set in order since the origin of the universe, that is continued through evolutions and still exists as a perfect compromise between living and the non-living? The complexities in anatomical and histological structures of human beings and the details within them are still not yet completely understood. Research only leads to certain theories and hypotheses of some incompletely understood concepts that get revised and re- revised by scientists without a fruitful result. No other idol, icon or soul could retain such a marvelous functioning of our universe, other than some mighty supernatural power.

Hence the existence of universe cannot be accidental and its survival cannot be a mere chance factor. It also remains a fact that nothing comes into being without a creator. Thus, even the existence of universe has to have a meaning and that meaning has to be understood to make our existence meaningful. If we do not try to understand the meaning of it then we will not be any different than the animals that are living for the sake of living. We have to understand, after seeing the signs of the maker and keeper of this universe, to justify our responsibility and our role as humans.

If we agree that there is an eternal power behind, then we need to know whether it is single or multiple. If it would have been multiple then the laws regulating the continuity of existence would have been different in different geographical zones. But the system of governance of the heavenly bodies, plant and animal kingdoms and properties of the non-living is one and the same. Then we are obliged to accept the creator as one, of course without partners. Henceforth, the need for faith in Monotheism.

On the other hand it is we who are governed by selfishly motivated interests and self made rules of comfort seeking that only when confronted with hardships and difficulties we resort to some unseen power for rescue and relief. There have been countless examples of non-believers or disbelievers who cry out to some supernatural power in times of depression or despair but, no sooner they are relieved of their suffering and agony they resume the irrational ideology of "there is no God" and return to selfish gratifications of personal needs so very conveniently placed before them, that they almost forget their innate dependence on mercy and kindness from the one almighty.

Curiously the teachings of other major religions, more importantly Christianity and Judaism also preach obedience to God's legislation and the same has been taught by many prophets of the past times. Immaterial of the presentations by different messengers and commandments from different religions of different times, the core interpretation of the context has been the same and that is, to submit ourselves totally to God's will to be on the right path, following the true creator and regulator of the universe, which is worshipping the almighty force. This mindset has to be framed first otherwise our subsequent actions, programmed to congeniality of living for a purpose cannot be rationalized.

As on today many religions exist and contradict each other because of their biased reasons. Wars were fought in the past and there are fights in the present for the same, oppression is continued by the dominants on the weaker sections when the fact remains that all religions have a single common origin and the entire mankind is just one universal brotherhood, the human nature remains the same from the beginning to the end. Hence all religions taught by all the prophets of all times, basically originated by the God.

But unfortunately the presented religions are confusing the man instead of guiding him and not satisfying the psychological, physical, spiritual needs of his. They should teach humans to discriminate good from the evil and right from the wrong. A religion should balance the life with hope, patience, honesty, courage, endurance, peace and security. Any religion which does not teach these basics is not a religion itself. A religion must express a purpose of its own and should justify the signs of God to induce faith.

QORAN described the formation of human beings and other living beings from mud and water. So in other words life was created from 'Dust' and this creation is rational in the light of present day science which is able to differentiate the cellular structure at the molecular level, to confirm that the most basic ingredients of life are actually atomic configuration of elemental forms. It has unfolded the scientific basis of cellular structure of the living unit as the basis of life, constituting the combination of inorganic and organic elements along with water, as a variant explanation for protoplasm.

The science of embryology only of late admitted human creation as a combination of sperm and ovum, already mentioned in last God-sent word as 'mingled fluids' referring to fertilized ovum and the growth of the embryo to fetus in the uterus, as a 'clinging entity' in the mother's womb, meant to be brought out as a separate life. The 'book' also mentioned about the creation of earth, mountains, oceans and plant kingdom and the governance of heavenly bodies, light, heat, atmosphere, climatic swifts and rainfall with 100% scientific accuracy though it is not a science manual. This truth was revealed and passed on to the mankind by the last messenger 1400 years back.

The purpose to send prophets in different eras was the need of the times and the same was fulfilled by revelation on the selected few to guide to the right path and thereby to allow the law and order to prevail, resultantly to implement harmony in societies.

There is not much debate regarding the hierarchy of prophets. The controversy however remained about the authenticity of different religions which were created. The importance of believing in God sent words faded and is responsible for invention of different forms of religion. This confusion of different values and virtues among different religions still prevailing in the world is for its own loss and consequent suffering.

We know our world is planet earth and the life on earth gives plenty of opportunity to the man-kind to seek the truth and to act accordingly, referring to the signs of existence of One almighty. The paradigm of faith as a prerequisite to practice a life of harmony benefits us. The order to worship God is not to bring about any solace to God, but brings about the required solace in the believers. The inheritance of wisdom from Prophet Adam, to Prophet Abraham, and Prophet Jesus and Prophet Moses is true and requires belief from all Muslims. Muslim means a believer of Islam and Islam directs total submission to one God.

The holy books Torah and Bible do not remain in their original forms, which are very well accepted by the believers of Christianity and Judaism. In other words they were tampered, as per their own claim, which makes them untrue in purity. Christian scholars themselves confided in the fabrications made by Paul, who also brought differences in Christian history and church doctrines. What so ever, original contents that remained in their books also pointed out and confirmed the oncoming Prophet Mohamed, which is clearly documented in their books of faith. It is the QORAN which was not fabricated by its memorization and methodology of preservation, out of unbroken living sequence of devotion of the believers nullifies the probability of change. Extensive research by famous non-muslim historians prove that QORAN till date remains exactly the same as the first copy.

All religions do believe that Jews and Arabs descended from Prophet Abraham, Jews from his son Isaac and Arabs from his son Ishmael, so both Jews and Arabs become brethren in literal sense. In Jewish doctrine a quotation is documented that "I will raise a prophet like you among the brethren", actually is referring to Prophet Mohamed and not to Prophet Jesus, because he was among themselves and not from their Brethren. Secondly the mention of 'one like you' refers to the similarities between Prophet Moses and Prophet Mohamed, both had similar lives, they were not raised in their parent's home, were married, had children, both migrated for their mission and both died natural deaths and all of this does not refer to Prophet Jesus.

Christians denote that Jesus was the son of God rooted in the scriptures of Bible, that Jesus called God as 'Father', but calling God as father does not imply that there exist a paternal relationship between the two and it only imparts a sense of respect and hence according to Mathews and John the name father was used figuratively and not literally. So Jesus could not have been a son of God, rather the virgin status of Mary and the miraculous birth of Jesus were miracles like many other miracles shown by God to many other Prophets in different ways.

Jesus was created as Adam was created by God from dust without fathers and when Christians agree that Adam was created without both Father and mother and when Allah could create such diverse and variant species of living beings from nothing, it would not have been difficult to create Jesus without a father. Hence birth of Jesus was just another sign of an unusual miracle done by almighty.

Moreover Jesus had dependence on biological needs from intake to output and from absorption to excretion; hence he could not have been different from any other human being with their limitations.

It becomes evident that there is no need for confusion about the fact that Jesus was not a son of God.

QORAN mentions the fundamental principle of TAWHID, one God and the need to submit ourselves in absolute totality to Him. That is the meaning of ISLAM and this amount of faith is a prerequisite, for being a Muslim. Worship cannot be initiated without the belief that there is no deity except 'Allah' and Prophet Mohamed was his messenger. Worship thereafter is to one and includes everything which is righteous- righteous beliefs, righteous deeds and righteous way of life.

Worship in Islam does not restrict itself to performance of prayers, fasting, charity and pilgrimage, worship is also choosing the righteous way of life by living in harmony with other fellow human beings, which includes taking care of family, relatives, neighbors, friends, acquaintances and strangers in that order of priority and sharing with the poor, orphans, travelers and the needy. Remaining patient during sickness, steadfast in times of stress and keeping up to promises is also worship in Islam. QORAN also advocates that being kind towards one's wife and sympathetic towards the deserving, helpful to the under privileged, affectionate towards one's children and meeting to one's commitments, is nothing but worship.

Work is a necessity and sincere work of performing duties dutifully is nothing but a very sophisticated kind of worship. Seeking knowledge is yet another form of worship, which is declared equivalent to duty. Knowledge has a high value and spending an hour in doing so is also considered equivalent to praying. None the less social courtesy and tolerant cooperation is given a great importance in the religion as a form of worship.

A simple task of helping each other and speaking softly to fellow humans is nothing but yet another way of worship, as it leads to resultant peace and harmony in every one's life and society in turn.

QORAN was a revelation to Prophet Mohamed which SAHABA memorized in his life time and one year after his death the copies of this document were sent to different countries for its presentation. Till date no copy of QORAN was found different from the other and it can only happen if it is preserved by God as was His promise.

The ritualistic pattern of performing SALAH is a mark of faith to be a Muslim. By doing this ritual we dislocate ourselves from our wordly activities five times a day to meditate and come into direct contact with the creator and the sustainer to seek help and guidance. The very fact that we have somebody to turn to for help and guidance is a solace in itself. Secondly turning to seek guidance makes oneself humble and modest in approach, which takes away the unwanted pride and prejudices from us and it is the most wanted behavior of a human being to survive in a society with harmony. It does a lot of good to one and all who practice this ritual. Thanking the almighty, five times a day for all the blessings showered on us creates a sense of fulfillment and contentment. The rigid regularity of timings of worship also brings about a discipline warranted for good living.

The ablution being a prerequisite indicates the importance of cleanliness and hygiene, yet another prerequisite for healthy living. The physical aspect of SALAH is a perfect example of stretching exercises; again well required for reducing the stress of living and to get a feeling of relaxation, mandatory to peaceful life. More importantly from the psychological point of view, it brings a distancing and displacement from our tensions and stress, which no amount of wealth, fame, honor or education could achieve.

Another pillar of Islam being the ZAKAH is indicative of the divine concept of socialism. It points out to the affirmation that everything bestowed on us is Allah's blessing, the assets and richness is endowed upon by Allah and we are only trustees to the same, so we are obliged to share with the other members of our society who are less fortunate and deserve a part of our riches. The divisibility of share in charity (as much as that can be afforded) is compulsory to be given to other deserving classes. Giving charity and alms is hence another form of worship, which in itself corrects the imbalances in classes thrust upon by the society and brings about stability in economics of the community. It also disintegrates the attitude of selfishness, which can harm oneself and so also diminishes an attitude of jealousy which otherwise could bud up harming the immediate interpersonal relationships.

Fasting during the month of Ramadan, SIYAM is yet another test of faith and an obligation which benefits the one who fasts. It is not merely refraining from eating or drinking, but also to restrain ourselves from all senses which derive pleasure, gratification and comfort of an individual. It makes us understand what deprivation of basic and human needs mean and infects a feeling of care and concern for those who are tested against these deprivations. It induces the strength of tolerance and forbearing in oneself and advocates a sense of sympathy and kindness for others, a very wanted quality for sustenance of congenial relationship in society. It also brings a deep insight into our own limitations and the importance of the provider.

Islam preaches universality of brotherhood and equality of racial position. HAJJ or pilgrimage to Mecca manifests a motivated practice to enact the same. Here one cannot differentiate between big or small, rich or poor, black or white skin and advises a congregation of all to assemble at one place and to show consideration for the rights of others, protecting one's rights at same time. It inhibits venturing into certain sanctioned rights for a particular period of time to inviolate the lives of animals and plants even, thereby extricating the violation of other species of living kingdom.

So pilgrimage to HAJJ is a simple teaching that exemplifies harmonious living among the living beings and the basic purpose of most of the philosophies, now celebrated as doctrines are actually following this teaching of equality and harmony. It is only at this time of congregation that you cannot make distinction between dress, physical appearance, wealth or wisdom among humans and Allah deals with all alike without discrimination to race, nation, tribe, caste or creed and to signify that all mankind has a common origin. It remains an indication of how Allah judges his creations to respect diversity among ourselves.

The diversity which no doubt exists is in the dialect, mannerisms, culture and traditions and this much of diversity is warranted for a congenial livelihood. Righteousness would remain righteousness. Righteousness in turn is observance of duty of submission to almighty, which in itself is the only solution to our problems and an answer to our confusion, unhappiness and purchased suffering.

Believers of all religions agree upon the age old saying that God helps those who help themselves, but this signifies only petty tasks which a man can do by himself. Beyond doubt there are aspects of life which we cannot help ourselves and are helped by some unknown factors and again beyond doubt it is not a matter of coincidence. Survival of the fittest is the nature's law for animal kingdom, which does not hold good for humans. If not for certain teachings of God the humans would have followed the same rule and would have perished. Instead humans have to be good, courteous and considerate towards other fellow beings while surviving as explained in QORANIC teachings.

To 'err' is human, an age old saying which has never been contradicted. Human beings are bound to 'err' and God gestures the understanding of this human weakness. But if it exceeds in quantity, quality and duration it becomes a sin. Almighty safeguards from the evils of the society, to avoid possibility of a continuous turmoil caused by selfishly motivated ordeals, which if not curbed will only jeopardize the comfortable existence of human beings themselves.

Humans depend on things [other than what they are supposed to seek refuge for], rely on favors from others and crave for blessings from those who are also dependent on others at some part of their lives in some form or other. This creates a chance for the wrong to occur and continue, increase and enlarge. Wrong is being a wrong witness, being oppressive and hurtful to others for our own good, and to not have a check on our greed, lust and wants.

Here comes the belief in the Day of Judgment, which signifies the final analysis of our deeds and actions [and the burden of such deeds is accountable on the quantum of the subsequent commitments] which forces the mankind to contemplate the limitations, to avoid bad behavior and which if intelligently done cannot only escape the punishment in hereafter but the punishments imposed by society. So if one doubts the Day of Judgment, in turn the existence of God, they doubt the eventualities not feeling responsible for their actions. QORAN tells us that there are signs of the existence of God around us and the Day of Judgment, and that almighty is the eternal authority to check on the mortals everywhere.

Creations other than humans are not empowered with a free will, and only we can exercise it to choose the path of righteousness and not of evil. Seeking guidance and education is for our own good and going astray is for own loss. Not seeking guidance and education is like disobedience to God. Guidance had been provided via Prophets in all eras. Only selected few can appreciate this blessing based on their level of intelligence. QORAN says in so many words 'that some are guided by Allah and some deservedly sent astray'.

Some refuse and reject the signs of God and prefer to live in ignorance, apparently engrossed in the worldly pleasures, but in fact are busy displacing a lack of contentment in their lifestyles. The concept of guidance is not that only those who possess faith are properly guided, but interestingly Allah extends His sympathies and guidance on all those who seek repentance and guidance from Him. QORAN says 'Allah guides those who turn to him in repentance'.

Now comes the need to explore the rightfulness of the belief in one God, who is beyond doubt a very generous provider, as the availability of the consumables have never ended and does not seem to exhaust even in future, except until the dooms day. Then comes the question of what to adopt for a peaceful living of the inmates of this universe. Which code of ethics is the best? Which ideology satisfies the universal flawless code to be true?

It is the human being that is created in the best form in comparison to other creations. The tact, the understanding, the capacity, the faculty, the strength and the intellect raises human beings to the privileged class among the living and keeps non-humans and non-living for the use, exploitation and comfort of this privileged class.

Theological arguments are distracting and even damaging at times, as they are immature, unrealistic and unimaginative for the kind of absolute certainty expected out of any understandable religion. But faith remains the prerequisite for the existence of God which gets proved throughout our lives that God exists and this existence is necessary for peaceful existence of human beings and other creatures. Religion teaches that egotism, greed and violence are wrong. Religion also teaches that one human is expected to be generous to another human and the dictum is 'do not do to others, what you would have not done to you'.

Man lives among the spiritual beings [angels] and physical beings [other creatures on earth] thus religion guides man to balance skills, demands, needs, desires and contentment, to bring a sense of organization in all walks of life, keeping a balance between physical and spiritual concepts.

The provider of basic needs necessary for life is one, just one controller and there are several ways and means of knowing the existence of one controller.

God sent messages were given to chosen people. They compiled them into books and it was the responsibility of mankind thereafter to convey the same to generations to follow with utmost truthfulness and sincerity, but it was not undertaken appropriately due to unforeseen reasons in case of ZUBUR and undertaken with vested interests fabrications in case of TORAH and BIBLE.

To judiciously execute this supreme task of passing on the truth, certain regulations become mandatory and these regulations were revealed to mankind from times immemorial through messengers and revelations from God in the form of God sent messages.

The scriptures sent before QORAN kept changing with passage of time and lost their originality, thereby violating the laws of God which warranted the need to send the last word of God to Prophet Mohamed in the form of QORAN. It documents the history of past prophets and previous books. God testified to preserve it in original form forever. It remains a fact that we witness even after 1400 years QORAN has remained the same and would sustain till the Day of Judgment as promised by God.

We are supposed to show abstinence from SHIRK (assigning partners to God), which is not expected out of us after all the favors given by Almighty. Curiously it is a curse to rely on subjects, objects, authorities, contacts and means of influence, other than God as it confabulates our expectancy levels and brings only time bound results, which even if clicks would lead to further dependence and would undermine one's coping resources, if it does not click would lead to rebound frustration and so also would shatter our confidence levels defeating the effort in itself.

The other imposed religious responsibilities called FARAID are no favors returned to the Almighty, as they only benefit ourselves and the society in which we live, those are rather for our own good. The enforced laws of religion are actually attributes in the best interests for a peaceful living. But for that we have to follow only one constitution and it is possible if we submit ourselves to the belief in one God almighty, which had been revealed messages from time to time.

On the contrary if there is diversity in the constitution to be followed, it would bring conflict in the expectations among followers resulting in poor thresholds of tolerance in some classes leading to disharmony, chaos and turmoil. Obedience to laws of one constitution only, broadens the demography of individual rights along with respect to other's rights. It would also discourage the evils of greed for more, wrong doings for selfish motives, envy towards the blessed and fear of uncertainty, thereby making every one more free, happy and comfortable with each other, otherwise the lawlessness would jeopardize the sustenance of peaceful society.

As man is given the superiority over the other creatures it remains his responsibility to keep a balance and peace in the world, more so because all others are inadvertently following the laws of governance prescribed by the nature and God anyways. The voluntary choice is given only to man to do as he wishes and to enact according to his choice and it becomes all the more important for man to follow the will of God, because quality of life of all living beings depends on the decisions between wrong or right deeds. Hence it becomes compulsory to restraint his wishes and desires to suit the existence of everything else in the universe. These laws are conveyed to the mankind by prophets chosen by God from time to time. 25 messengers are documented in QORAN, some were sent to the same place at the same time as other messengers, but there were innumerable more chosen for the same purpose, at other tours and places.

4 God sent words were later compiled into books and revealed to prophet Abraham as chronicles, prophet David as Zubur, prophet Moses as Torah and prophet Jesus as Bible other than Prophet Mohamed who received the last testament in the form of QORAN. All are the words of God in the form of messages sent and resent to different chosen few, in different parts of the words at different times.

All messages convey that good deeds will be rewarded and bad deeds will suffer punishments, but this fact is not imbibed or felt as an eventual happening, thus irregularities exist in the form of sinful becoming prosperous and righteous suffering, guilty escaping punishments and innocents getting culminated.

The deserved returns of actions have to be faced sooner or later. If not obvious to our perceptions, the results are seen in some other form and the order is maintained. So our job is to submit to the God and to worship. Worship means living a normal life with a purpose, the purpose is to undertake our duties, our duties are our responsibilities which are directed by the almighty. If we do not get the expected returns, it only indicates the purpose and need for our betterment. Believe that everything happens for the good of it. But we are expected to think, plan and work to achieve it according to our capacity, which vary from person to person and rest remains our destined fate. Fate is our destiny governed by God and events happen to us, as already known to God only.

Man thinks that gratification of needs is the sole purpose of life given to him but, the true purpose of life is to repay the provider his blessings enabling us to get gratification of both physical and mental needs, by worship. Worship is not just obeying the commands but it is also not escaping from the liabilities given to one. Man has to build rational wisdom and spiritual faculty, which will get him reward in the form of ranks. Ranks come with responsibilities. The more rewarding a rank one gets, the more responsible and diligent he has to be to satisfy it.

Thus he is made accountable for his acts on achieving maturity. Each human bears the brunt of its actions and continues responsible for working out his salvation. Ranks are demarcated to encourage efforts and fulfillment of responsibilities associated with the ranks, which is no big a deal if one commits to one's duties.

Every person born is in accordance with the intra uterine growth pattern according to the will of God and every person's fate is destined according to his IQ level, his talents, his capabilities and his potential, which remains predetermined by the environment he is made to face during his pre and post natal life.

Accountability is reached after mental maturity and then each person has to bear the burden of his responsibility and consequence of his actions. To guide the human race towards the correct path several prophets were sent, which is documented in history. Those who have no means of knowing the true religion but have followed the correct guided by common sense, and those who know the truth are expected to spread the truth among others, otherwise subjected to questioning.

The human nature is more reformative than a hopeless asset and blind faith is not advised, rather one's satisfaction has to be reasonably founded on well understood convictions. Islam insures freedom of belief, which eventually leads to faith in God. One has to believe in QORAN as God sent word and traditions of Prophet Mohamed as practical implementations of QORANIC principles.

Faith is the absolute knowledge and acceptance of God, His angels, His book as God sent message, Mohamed as His last prophet and the day of final judgment to come. The confidence in these articles has to be unshakable. One also has to share his wealth, time, health, knowledge and experience acquired as a gift from God with others. One is also obliged to fathom the rewards given by God in prayers regularly thanking him, which naturally instills humbleness and steadfastness.

One also has to part away with wealth in charity to the beneficiaries individual or organizational, which is two and half percent of annual income or total value of assets after discounting expenses and credits. One also has to refrain from doing wrong and disallow others to do so and practice speaking the truth, engaging in good talk and allowing others to do the same. One has to read and understand God's message in QORAN and prophet's quotations with absolute humility. One also has to love God, Prophets, love the fellow human beings and lastly has to show kindness towards neighbors, kith, kin and guests. God also forbids doing any harm to others especially to the neighbors. He wants you to remain kind towards the guests and strangers visiting your domain. Thus faith is deep penetration into life's meaning and strong resistance against returning to disbelief.

Faith encompasses personal, social, political, financial and spiritual fields of life. Sinful behavior is becoming of humans.

Sins were classified as big or small. Firstly sins against God and secondly sins against the fellow humans. Sins against God are directly related between the person and the creator and are considered forgivable upon God's discretion except creating partner to God. To the extent that an atheist will also be forgiven if he turns to God in the lifetime. God is merciful in forgiving sins only if pardon is asked truthfully. But sins against the humans are forgivable if and only if the concerned person forgives or if the offender is willing to give reasonable compensation to the victim or his family. Thus it is well documented that Sin is acquired and not in born and if some act is done out of mere natural instincts or uncontrollable urges then God understands the human nature more than anybody else, but man's responsibility will be questioned as he is also taught to be patient and tolerant towards his own instincts and urges which may cause inconvenience to others.

Religion should address to human conditions of the present and for the destiny thereafter, because He created and designed the world for a purpose. Man is created and commissioned to be the God's viceroy on earth. So the purpose has to be served by the man to cultivate goodness, enrich knowledge and to give meaning to the life.

The beginning of mankind with the well known historical events of repentance from Adam and Eve, then the forgiveness given by the creator was actually to teach discipline, to differentiate good from the evil, to experience the fall and rise of position and to understand straying away and asking pardon followed by reconciliation with the God. The event also highlights that both Adam and Eve were equally tempted, responsible, and remorseful and were forgiven, that both are equal but not identical and that man has a free will to undertake deeds for which he is answerable. The free will of the man should also allow him to guard his integrity, preserve his identity, and observe the commands of the God and also to fulfill his social obligations.

Religion is expected to teach to love fellow beings for the sake of God, which denotes social well being to get rest assured. One is expected to speak truth and abstain from telling lies, and to be transparent in dealings with others, thereby fraud and cheating are curbed by itself bringing peace in society. Such teachings are learnt by the quotations recorded from the Ahadith of the Prophet. The limited words, packed in a volume of a single book may not encompass all the complexities of living and dealings expected out of a community with different roles and different liabilities, so the path followed by the Prophets have become words which lead, guide and answer certain queries.

Religion teaches repeatedly that certain actions are not considered righteous and may even tantamount to contradiction of faith like making partners to God. Faith also directs us to certain actions contrary to our liking but mandatory for social well being and that is to spend one's wealth among the kith and kin, for the benefit of orphans and for the advantage of the needy and also for those who ask from you. Faith will be incomplete if we do not remain firm and patient in times of pain and suffering. Our actions have to be shown openly like in charity and kindness towards fellow human beings, as it would support the system and flourish the society letting others to follow suit and to do good to the community. Feeling good within is also an achievement which promotes repetitive behavior of the same and is becoming of a strong faith with constant practice.

Believing and enacting the main principle from the God sent word allows peace in oneself, security to the family and harmony in the society so also solidarity of the nation at large.

Certain directives enforce individuals to react to the needs of the helpless, to fulfill commitments towards the exploited and to alleviate their sufferings letting them live peacefully, enjoyably and contentedly. If is done with some regularity can even become a habit thereby creating a society without frustrations, anxieties and depressions.

Piety is yet another quality warranted out of human beings, which will be completed if a person is willing to spend in the name of God, out of what is provided to him by God. He also should be able to restrain anger and should be able to pardon others for their mistakes. He should remain steadfast in times of hardships and to feel remorse after committing wrong doings and to ask for forgiveness. A pious human being is one who is not persistent in committing mischief after having been forgiven. The other qualities of righteousness are being able to perform self control of anger and other volatile emotions, to be able to remain patient, tolerant and considerate and to show strong will power and complete abstinence from animate provocations.

One is expected to believe in the distinction between the QORAN and SUNNAH, the first being the God sent word and the second being the practical implementation of QORAN, by the prophet Mohamed. It should be realized that both are in complete harmony with each other. As man is reformable, prophets were sent in all ages to enlighten the path of righteousness. One is expected to get true guidance first and then is held responsible for their deeds and wrong doings. Then punishment becomes mandatory for the good will of society.

A man's life then becomes a gift of God he is supposed to cherish it with pleasures, achievements and also should compromise with frustrations out of sufferings and failures. But self destruction and killing by suicide is forbidden, because life is a transit to the eternal life thereafter. So life has to be spent with certain principles concerning lives of one and the others, to live and let live in peace.

The concept of sin is age old, even dating back to the era of Adam and Eve, the Garden of Eden gifted to them, the imposition to avoid a particular tree, the human urge and curiosity, misdirection from evil falling on them and their eviction to the earth. Their ultimate apology to God and bestowed forgiveness, is a lesson to the mankind to enjoy the given by remaining contended and to refrain from the forbidden. It also highlights the nature of human beings with insatiable urges and their proneness to commit mistakes or sins.

It should also be known that committing sins and asking for forgiveness does not necessarily bring reform or restrict the provisions given by God. But committing sins with the plan of seeking forgiveness is not acceptable by any law and religion. It is exemplary that even prophets have committed mistakes, as to err is human, but the question of remorse and to ask for forgiveness also indicates the insight one develops about the right and the wrong, plus the sensibility to recognize the good from the evil.

A new born for example cannot commit mistakes or sins, so it is the post natal life with its external forces and environmental influences, like the home atmosphere which dictates the behavior, sins or evil doings. Science admits that the first set of emotional experiences that a child learns is discrimination between self and non self, trust, love and then control of urges. The genetic influences which the present day science explains is only up to the extent of revealing the predispositions, which of course can be modulated by concrete and abstract intelligence, which always is divided into the inborn and learned intelligence and can differentiate the overt and covert learning.

God has inflicted a system in which the spirit of perfection, justice, wisdom, mercy and compassion are imbibed into the human nature and a man is supposed to retain at least some portions of the above. But again how good and perfect a man may be, he cannot stand equal or rival to his creator, because the amount of such qualities are negligible in comparison to God. Man is expected to understand the revelations of God, support reason, seek freedom with limitations and achieve goodness.

The challenges of struggle endowed upon us by God, actually make life interesting and devoid of monotonous stagnation. A man is imperfect but imperfection is not a sin, as sin is what is done deliberately, sin is denying the laws of nature, violating other's rights and inflicting intentional harm to fellow human beings repeatedly. But the intrinsic capacity to sin is not greater than the capacity to privy. What is expected is possible and within man's reach.

The concept of freedom is also misunderstood and abused, as no man can be totally free within the confines of a society, because if the society has to function man has to have certain limitations around his freedom. Freedom is given to believers as well as for the non believers equally. So a man remains free unless he violates the laws of God or of the fellow human beings.

There is no scope for superstition, uncertainty, corruption or disorder. It is also pointed out that there is no necessity for the religion also to be compelled on those who do not delineate truth from the error. As religion is based on faith, belief and commitment will become meaningless if forced against somebody's will. The choice is left on the man to take its own course and he is solely responsible for his actions either to reap the fruits or to purchase punishment. So there is no room for religious persecution, conflict in classes and racial prejudices.

All mankind has similar cellular biology, molecular chemistry and biophysics created by God and God is kind to all, as they all belong to him. Hence there will be no place for atrocities or exploitations from one to the other and there will be no scope for social classes or privileged races and subsequently chance of oppression. The distinction is brought about by individual merits and deeds. Then again all mankind is supposed to hold brotherhood for one another.

All mankind is equal but not identical, as there could be differences of individual capabilities, IQ levels, asset values and ambitions, but there does not exist any superiority from one to the other, which is also recognized by science. The distinction which will be taken into account is that of piety, goodness and righteousness. Whereas the difference in the color caste, creed, stature and race remain incidental and discrimination is not acceptable in religion.

All men have same creation and same destiny. No one can carry any worldly belongings with him in the end and will ultimately have to return to him. Faith confers that all messengers were sent by God and there is no discrimination between one or the other, with the fact that Prophet Mohamed was the last messenger to humanity.

Peace is another prerequisite which is warranted out of religion. Prayers and salutations are expressions of peace. So a man has to be in peace with him and others, in which case all types of relationships will be characterized by coherence, intimacy, equality and integrity. Because man in not completely independent and societies are intertwined, communities can entertain people via activities and experience a perfect harmony. That is why a crisis on a member displaces its burden on the rest. Hence in religion a community is not founded on the basis of location, occupation or kinship.

Community has broader concept of national and political extensions and demands good for all. So a man is expected to know what to accept and what to reject. There has to be a balance in principles, conduct, unity, solidarity, equity and continuity of community. There are rules for holding responsibilities of marriage, there are duties towards charity, rights for others, and obligation towards our children, family and neighbors. And for that matter performance of certain rituals in unison during HAJJ are orientations towards continuity of a healthy community.

The concept of morality does not make one accountable for anything beyond ones scope or power. Everything is permissible and few things are obligatory. When obedience to administration is mandatory, then obedience to the creator naturally becomes compulsory. Morality also differentiates the values like humbleness, simplicity, courtesy and compassion which please the God from vices like arrogance, pride, vanity, harshness and indifference that are not liked by the God. So a Muslim is expected to show kindness to the kin, concern for the neighbors, respect for the elderly, love towards the youngsters, care for the sick, support to the needy, sympathy to the distressed, patience with those that need guidance, and to express tolerance towards the ignorant.

Religion advocates us to be honest, perfect, knowledgeable, achievers and rectifiers of mistakes committed by self or others. We are asked to repent for our sins, feel responsible, be mindful for others and provide dependents for their legitimate needs, we are obliged to keep our eyes open and do research for community's progress.

We are instructed to follow certain regulations like, to believe in one God and Prophet Mohamed as his last messenger, to pay our due taxes every year as ZAKAT, to fast in the month of Ramadan, to make pilgrimage to Mecca once in a lifetime, to dress well in the places of worship, to eat and drink what is permissible, to not waste or excess, we are instructed to refrain from intoxicating drinks HARAM meat [meat from animals which are not slaughtered properly] and asked not to eat flesh of swine, wild animals, birds which use claws, teeth or beaks to kill and eat prey; and the dead animals. We are prohibited from gambling, having relationships other than that of a wedlock, dressing, walking or talking immodestly.

All these are necessary ordinances to bring discipline in self, harmony in society and to ward off evil and illnesses. These prohibitions can be exempted by God in two extra ordinary situations like, emergencies and acts committed in total ignorance or innocence.

We are restricted from committing shameful acts in public or sins big or small, from going against reasoning, discussing about God's matters, which we are not sure of, wasting provisions in excess, exhibiting and showing off, disrespecting parents, depriving children of their righteous needs and being hypocrites.

We should believe that our assets and incomes are God's gifts and God provides living for you as well to others through you. God burdens souls only with so much which they can shoulder.

We are also obliged to be just in business, avoid assault even if angered, speak truth, not to break oath after confirmation, invite others to the path of righteousness, to debate gracefully and not argue, to accept the destiny as God rewards people according to their merit of performance, to learn to pardon and forgive, to conduct joint affairs of betterment by mutual consultation, to spend judiciously out of bestowed wealth to defend oppression and not to yield to cruelty, to inhibit those who defy justice and transgress other's rights.

If we seek transitory material pleasures they will be granted only by God, but pending tests. But those who care less for the material pleasure of present days will be appreciated by God. We should be kind towards our parents and should not antagonize them, rather speak to them with honor.

We should give the rights to the needy. We should not spend our wealth lavishly neither be a miser. We should refrain from adultery, as it is a sin which would lead to other sins. We should take care of orphan's property and improvise, till they attain an age of full strength. We should complete the given words and undertake the agreements truthfully; otherwise we will be questioned on the day of reckoning. We should deal in business with utmost honesty and when we measure we must weigh it with a straight balance, as it will be advantageous for both the parties.

We should avoid arguing on matters about which we have no knowledge. We should be aware of the fact that our intentions and acts will be known by God and will be enquired thereafter. We should not be arrogant or express pride, as we have limitations in our capabilities. We should not hate others as it is evil to do so. We should show gratitude towards mothers, as they bear us and bring us up. We should also be considerate with the non-believers. We should keep our voice low in conversions and be moderate in our attitudes.

Intoxicants and gambling are forbidden for our own good, as we will only prosper if we show abstinence from them. We have to be contended with the portion which is destined in this world and refrain from doing any mischief as God does not like it.

These principles should be enforced completely and effectively, as they in turn will help the follower in achieving a strong moral character and personality strengths.

If we are oppressed or wronged by others, then either we fight for our rights by resisting and retaliating in equal measure or forgive the sinners and leave the results to God.

By fighting for our rights we are helping to establish order and justice. If forgiveness would have been advised alone, then there was the chance for the wrong doers to continue and even to exceed the limits, so God has kept room for mercy, patience, spirituality and morality, but total and continual forgiveness is not in the interest of the humanity in the long run, hence by advocating both the ways in practice, wrong doers who are repeating the oppression will benefit by granted pardon and those who are prone to pursue the wrong course, retaliation will curb their behavior and in turn would arrest the evil. So forgiveness in spite of allowance to retaliate is genuine forgiveness and hence perpetuates similar allowance for reform by the wrong doers.

CHAPTER 2

I slam's thrust on ideological application also includes quest for knowledge, experiment, observation, research and meditation to acquire sufficient experience to achieve wisdom. Faith in existence of God cannot be attained through mere imitation of rituals or formal acceptance. Faith encourages man to implement his intellect and wisdom with seriousness, as Islam identifies with intelligence quotient.

A lifestyle with manners which encourages sound thinking and refreshes the mind is advised, such that they do not hamper the fulfillment of other obligations. Gambling with its unpredictable losses and subsequent tension is not permitted and similarly alcohol consumption which is prone to cause temporary loss of touch with reality and dependence and tolerance in the long run, when one finds difficulty to live without it and when one has to increase its quantity to get the desired effect is also forbidden for our own good.

Family values are given great importance in Islam. It emphasizes execution of duties towards one another, attempts to sustain continuity of peace among the family members and also provides affection and security for the dependents. Duties have to be performed as a moral responsibility and legal commitment. Ideals of other philosophies and mythologies now admit that there is no better way of glorious survival of society other than the unit of marital relationship, with children as fruits, and of course the duty by elderly parents has to be reciprocated judiciously.

A woman's needs are equally legitimate and warrant serious consideration towards her economic security, to which she was accustomed before marriage. Importantly there is no expectation on a woman to do the so called obligatory routine household work. Religion expects a marital bond to be kept as permanent as humanly possible, conditional to adequate compatibility, goodwill, consent, guardianship and judicious discretion of casual and intentional deviations. Islam also points to a favor of God that this bond is not in-dissolvable if it becomes disagreeable in terms of its sacramental and contractual meaning, so if it is not working out for genuine reasons, then it can be terminated with due equity and honor.

Importance is given to the roles of both husband and wife to remain generous and kind towards each other for a happy and fulfilling life. They are not to cause any harm or suffering to each other if consummation is not taking place and to be honorable in letting each other free of the bondage. The misconception about the QORANic verse that men are ordained to rule over wives stems from the restriction imposed upon men to act as trustees, guardians and protectors of wives again to the extent of within confines of division of labor and delineation of familial roles. It does not refer to any superiority of males over females, as both the genders are considered equal but not identical in the eyes of God.

A husband's obligation is to maintain family's needs like boarding, lodging, clothing, nourishing, caring and for overall well being in accordance to the normal standards of lifestyle, which a woman was accustomed to before marriage but keeps in consideration the capacity of a man earnings, assets and profession, neither with extravagance nor with misery, as two extremes. A husband is obliged to provide love, respect and kindness, maximum gratification to his wife with due consideration to her health by adopting decency in fulfillment of his desires. In absence of the above a wife can seek freedom from marriage.

Wife on the other hand has to give comfort, solace and support to her husband. She is obliged to be faithful, honest and trustworthy. She is expected to provide love, sexual intimacy to her husband and to avoid jealousy and maintain integrity. She should make herself desirable, attractive, responsive and cooperative. She has to protect her husband's belongings and trust in his absence and is not supposed to entertain strangers in the house in his absence.

With regards to the relationship between parents and children, both should not do any harm to each other. Parents should not be overprotective nor negligent. Children if not reared with balance can prove a false security or rather a source of distress with magnified temptations to 'err'. Parents should not be overconfident, bear false hopes and allow misdeeds by children. Religion recognizes parental role in formation of a child's personality. Parents should take good care of legitimate rights, educational needs and social welfare.

Religion conveys the concept of EHSAAN denoting the parental role for patience, compassion, counsel, and empathy towards children. EHSAAN also encompasses the children's role of obedience, submissiveness, support, maintenance and responsibility towards parents. Exemptions to the rule are if parents prove wrong and improper towards their duties to God.

There are set obligations towards others, including servants, relatives, friends and neighbors, they are obligations of brotherhood, help, justice, mercy, accommodation and dignifying the humanity without expecting reciprocation from others. Labor is honored and authority discharged with control. These directives are from the God only and not to expect reciprocation of similar roles from others. Neighbors enjoy a special privilege of being kept safe and secure. They must be taken as one's own family. The belief of a true Muslim is under jeopardy if one sleeps stomach-full while a neighbor is awake hungry.

Exchange gifts, presents and food delicacies with neighbors, share joys and sorrows with them. They deserve relief, concern, nursing care and consolation at the times of need. As an attention to detail, there are instructions not to disturb neighbors with noise or environmental pollution, rather their share of light and breeze should not be blocked, by constructing high rise buildings.

There should not be any show of superiority, power or wealth by any individual towards the society. Rather everyone should be taken as a member of universal family derived from Adam and Eve, as equal to a common parentage. Pitiful that only now the world is implementing the doctrine of 'no to racism', which was explained by QORAN 1400 years before. The diversity of caste, creed, color and race in only incidental and has no bearing in front of God.

QORAN demands decent labor as a duty of virtue and work as worship. It is considered a sin to remain dependent for livelihood, other than being a social stigma and receiving disgraceful humility. One should be self-supporting, enjoin any kind of work and discourage beggary. Muslims should enjoy freedom of enterprise and grope for opportunities to progress. Whatever one earns, saves or spends is one's own wish, except the mandatory liability of paying the due taxes to the state, which is a must. Thereby an individual brings prosperity to the state and state in turn has to provide security.

An employed person should work efficiently for his employer in turn getting entitled to a fair wage for his service. Business dealing should be straightforward, transparent and honest. Weights should be established with justice and wealth acquired by lawful means only. Cheating, exploiting, shortchanging and monopolizing are acts of sin and taking interest on money is even a bigger sin. It is important to realize that the owner and provider of amenities is God only and proprietor is a mere agent to impart the business deal.

QORAN considers possession of wealth as a trying test, whereby one becomes more answerable as to how he acquired, how he spent it and how he shared it. One has to be moderate in spending as per QORANIC verse, 'squander not your wealth in the manner of a spendthrift, which is an evil act'. One has to fulfill his obligations towards his fellowmen, like love for fellow human beings, mercy towards animals, kindness towards children, respect towards elders, consolation to the distressed, comfort to the sick and relief to the grieved.

One is supposed to keep clean and to consume a diet in moderate quantity with certain exceptions like forbidding meat of dead animals, flesh of swine, and consumption of alcohol and lifestyle of gambling. Curiously medical science of present day verifies the benefits of these prohibitions.

Clothing with decency and modesty, with emphasis on keeping away from certain items for men to impersonate women like golden jewels, pure silk, gems and stones, which only suits the feminine nature, as keeping the ordained identity is good for peaceful existence of society. Women are expected to maintain their chastity and dignity, for QORAN advised them to lower their gazes and to guard their chastity for it would curtail vanity, pride and unwanted esteem, which can as well reciprocate similar emotions in others, with consequent unhealthy competition and resultant punishment.

Politically Islam stood out as a different paradigm since it guided thorough sovereignty in the state. The ruler happens to be an acting executive chosen by the people to implement the law of God. The aim is to administer equal justice to all, regardless of race, caste or creed and the concept of minority does not arise neither does the concept of political parties with different manifestos come up, as only the law of God prevails with the administrator to justify rules for people at large.

Obedience to rulers is conditional to their obedience to God and rulers only having been chosen, on their merits of fitness, competence and virtues. Richness, family heritage and individual status do not hold any privilege for God and cannot be a merit for public offence. Even the electorate has to be aware of the public events and needs to cast their ballot after careful evaluation of the candidates, thereby becoming responsible citizens.

Similarly any ruler who betrays the law set by God for people, should be ousted out of the office and replaced by another who is fair to the people. So Islam discourages monarchy by inheritance, and governance of lifetime. The ruler is given dual responsibility, one towards God and another towards the people. There is room for legislative councils and advisory bodies to impart guidance and also to seek suggestions from a common man. Ruler must seek advice of wise people on different matters pertaining to conflicts of interest among the people.

Islam permits freedom of thought and expression, but also respects majority's opinion to be followed. The so called religious minorities' and groups that are protected by the state, need to pay ZAKATH or JIZYA tax due to the Government.

In regards to relations with other states, both Islamic and non-Islamic nations, the command is to have due respect for other faiths. Peace and goodwill missions should be sent and enacted for the sake of humanity. Islam is also intolerant to torture towards prisoners of wars. So Islamic states have a big role to play for the humanity at large.

It is natural for any person of normal intelligence to feel that certain distorted concepts in Islam [which prevail among non-believers about certain issues] like JIHAD (holy wars), NIKAH UL MUJTHIMAH (polygamy or plurality of wives, TALAQ (divorce from husband) and QADA UL NISA (status of women) do not deserve any explanation but warrant clarifications for the confused, advice for the critical minds and guidance for the misinformed Muslims, who are equally responsible to understand the true virtues of Islam.

Islam does not tolerate aggression, violence, hostility and harm to be caused to others and recommends fighting to curb and suppress such acts as a last resort.

The meaning of Islam is equivalent to peace, it preaches peace and if others are indifferent or non-aggressive, to remain discrete and not to wage any war. Simply put Islam did not spread by the sword or forceful inactions or compulsion to acceptance, as religion believes in introspection before accepting any religion and QORAN advocates not to get into dispute with other religions especially with Jews or Christians, they being AHL AL KITAB (followers of God sent books). History documents that Prophet Mohamed initially had to preach privately and not publicly in the best interests of lives of the new converts which were jeopardized. Only later Islam was propagated openly as commanded by God.

Prophet Mohamed and his followers were subjected to torture, persecution and confiscation of properties, forced separation from their families and other evil methods to stop preaching Islam. History also records that Quraiysh of Mecca had applied ostracism against Muslims, who were forced to inhibit themselves, were unable to interact with others and pressurized persecution increased to the extent that the infidels planned to kill Prophet to eliminate Islam. A time came when Prophet Mohamed was forced to immigrate to Medina, where he could preach in peace and even had to make treaties with non-Muslims for peace and reform.

Meccans then performed raids looting to harass Medinians and also instigated the non-Muslims of Medina to rebuke, and to cause unrest. Muslims were threatened from with-in and from outside and continued defending, resisting the aggression to bring tranquility and only thereafter that wars started for the sake of survival to regain freedom, to reunite with their families and to collect their belongings ultimately to regain peaceful existence, which followed a series of triumphs by fighting a fair and righteous war. Muslims conquered neighboring territories to start living side by side with the defeated non-believers in peace. Critics who could not deny the history started adopting the trend that Islam did not spread by force and suppression, but Islamic wars were waged for economic reasons and not reiterating the historical facts that war was declared by Romans and Persians first during the crusades of Middle Ages for religious circumstances.

QORANIC message to believers was 'invite to the way of God by wisdom and argue in the most gracious manner while preaching', but unfortunately in those times the only method of propagation of peaceful mission was by direct contact and personal dealing, for which preachers had to cross borders in protected groups. This method having misinterpreted as military intrusion can be easily described as non-military because Muslims did not cross borders all at one time, rather they did it in small groups in various directions at different times and succeeded in their preaching. Those who did not convert were only asked to pay ZAKATH or JIZYA for the administration of the law of God for the progress of the state they were living in, and to treat them as equals to any Muslim who was paying ZAKATH for the warranted economic support for governance.

The law of the land was simply enforced for the common man, to either accept Islam by free will or to stick to their own faith but remain as loyal citizens of the land and share equal rights. Now the liability falls on the critics to do research to prove how much did Muslims make money for themselves and how much money they invested in the revenues of the invaded territories for administration with peace and harmony, how much money was received by the central governance in Arabia and how much was the population ratio to the per capita income of the inhabitants and if so, was it worth the adventures in foreign land. Lastly how much economic prosperity followed the spread of Islam into the conquered regions and how much stress and difficulty the governance faced to establish the same.

Coming to the criticism on plurality of wives, since times immemorial the practices of Polygamy or Polyandry or other types of plural marriages had been a common place occurrence, the commonest being Polygamy, which was permitted in other religions like Polygamous Jewish immigrants, Afro-Asian bishops, Roman catholic mate swapping and Hindu 'Kamasutra' practices etc. and Polygamy by patriarchs, kings, governors and even by common man, practiced secretly or openly. In times of Biblical revelations Polygamy was accepted religiously and socially, (e.g.: the 10-virgins' story mentioned in Bible) not to mention with various interpretations. In Islam only Polygamy was permitted with certain terms, conditions and reservations for the eradication of certain evils like social problems of prostitution, infidelity, fornication, mate swapping, sexual laxity and homosexuality.

QORANIC guidelines were to the benefit of eradication of these social evils and permissibility of plurality of marriages with strict implementation of the order to sanction equal rights to the allowed four wives in treatment, provisions, support, protection and justice, with emphasis to marry widows or orphans or divorced women who were neglected else restricted marriage to one wife only. So QORAN neither introduced nor encouraged Polygamy.

The fact cannot be denied that statistics of the past and present revealed the disparity of number of females to males and the ratio of women to men, showing women outnumbering men since long. The explanation is the risks to life of men, in accidents, natural calamities, wars and prevalence of diseases. Science on the other hand corroborates medical foundations of hormonal insurgencies of males, feminine inhibitions in nature of females which had been the cause and effect of Polygamy since ages.

Marital relationships with discord find ways to seek consolation and gratification of emotional and physical needs from outside the marriage, which is made easy by the disparity of male-female ratio, no doubt causing illegitimacy, abortions, medical termination of pregnancies and other medico- legal problems.

Allowance of plurality of marriage in these pretexts remains to be the best alternative as extension of religious and legal rights to the women without corrupting the society by allowing illegitimate relationships or affairs. Women's need for a family refers to the desirable companionship of moral, sentimental, emotional, natural and social belonging to a family and children.

The science of psychology opinioned high threshold of tolerance, low expectancy levels and adjustable interpersonal relations among women folks and their gross dependence for security and stability through bonded partnerships, in absence of which woman becomes prone to psychological ailments like anxieties, depressions, obsessions, neurasthenia, premenstrual tensions and menopausal syndromes.

Islam directs men to marry a second wife only if they can fulfill all obligations to both wives with good reason and justification and to discourage hypocrisy or even diplomacy. Curiously this would appear antagonistic to women's liberation movement of present times. Critics trying to highlight the exploitation of the existing wives who they claim would be forced to accommodate, share and divide their husband's attention against their wishes, but they are not aware of the general welfare of Islam's outlook also to consider the feelings of those outnumbered unfortunate women and their rights at the same time, which may get disrupted if not attended to with sincerity.

If a marriage is without consummation, making the family life incomplete and disallowing preservation of human race and heritage much required for fundamental sustenance of family. The alternative of such a situation was divorce only because the wife could not give birth, which is not healthy and not encouraged in the religion, as it appears to be against natural aspirations of any one's rights. Moreover divorce on non-consummation need not be wife's fault, even if some etiological diagnostic criterion surfaces and secondly because it could as well be some undiagnosed sexual dysfunction in males which at any other time may not remain fruitful with other companions and it may not satisfy the wishful thinking of any man.

Adoption does not hold a solution in itself in the sphere of security, prosperity and substitution for natural guardianship and cannot satisfy the norms of extended love and care, being the outcome of relationship otherwise. The crisis intervention as regards to child psychology about the abstinence of the knowledge of original parentage can undermine the personality growth and the problems of inheritance and legal rights may remain unsolved.

Such practice can exceed the limit in any society by certain exploiters to seek allowance of 'sale' of children by some disordered parents, who may possibly be abusing them and in case of adoption of orphans, it may instigate irresponsible actions and unwanted intimacies, which cannot be accepted by nature and so discouraged in religion. Contrary to such measures allowance of another marriage will secure the lives of widows or divorcées or needy women and will strengthen the family ties of a community and weaken the disparity of socio-economic classes and may administer equality recommended by Islamic society.

Instances have been known, when obligations of wives, were not fulfilled due to illness or other reasons, jeopardizing the sublimation of manly needs, which should be satisfied in a respectable way, otherwise accidents of acquaintances turning into physical relations are a commonplace and with passage of time can cause disruption of family values and may also harm, hurt and demoralize other family members, in turn creating a turmoil of social norms.

Marriage in Islam is not just a contract between two partners, but is designated as moral charity, social integrity, psychological stability, spiritual peace and human mercy for two individuals to share in times of happiness and sorrow. The involved persons are supposed to know each other with preference given to piety, heritage, assets and appearance in that order of preference.

Woman's free will and consent is a necessity, she has to be given "MEHER" in the presence of two witnesses and marriage registered as an official document.

If marriage is not serving its purpose then it should be terminated with conservation of all rights, but giving a fair trial to the following means: All disputes to be settled first, arbitrators from both sides try mediation for compromise and only then divorce enacted in the most graceful manner. Divorce is not only the right given to a man, but woman can also exercise the same option and can seek it from husband and if he does not agree even on justifiable grounds, then court or QAZI can exercise the right to pronounce divorce.

After the divorce a waiting time of 3 months is given to woman, during which time it remains the liability of the husband to give maintenance to the woman. Allowance of divorce is an expression of God's intent of disapproving a life with marital discord. As both men and women are considered equal but not identical and woman in no manner taken as inferior to man. Men are not supposed to dominate women, except that men are ordained to take over the charge of women only as trustees, providers and caretakers.

The fabrication of history and labeling Eve only as culprit of mistake for having driven away from Heaven is not true. QORAN says both Adam and Eve were tempted, both committed to error, both sinned and both were forgiven and pardoned. Woman's role in Islam is no less vital than man, she having been given equal share in every aspect of responsibility. Women were also given rewards for deeds in pursuit of knowledge and education, entitled for equal freedom of expression, participation in public affairs including wars and were given equal rights to work, enterprise and returns.

Women were also awarded share from inheritance as half of that of men, since man is given the sole responsibility for maintenance of family and woman is made financially secure in all relationships pertaining to husband or wife, brother or sister, mother or son and father or daughter.

Woman is exempted from fasting, praying everyday prayers or the obligatory Friday prayer in congregation during menstruation. Being mother, she is entitled to more than fathers love from their children. Woman can retain whatever she possessed before marriage and she was given equal participation in work of any kind she could perform, with suitability to her feminine nature.

Women were asked to stand behind men during congregational prayers only to disallow mixing of both genders for obvious reasons and to disallow distractions to men. The usage of veil or HIJAB is again in her best interests to suit feminine nature and to disallow notoriety. HIJAB does not mean just a head scarf; it means to have a shield or protection by dressing modestly.

Righteous path can never bring bad results and wrong path can never bring good results. Righteous way as per the directives of QORAN, will also bring right thinking and right actions; in turn will bring peace of mind and good health. Right thinking is our responsibility and can help us overcome difficulties in our life.

Man acts as he thinks and the sum of all the thoughts, spontaneous or deliberate shape one's character and purity of thoughts will bring joy and peace. Noble conduct does not come by chance; it has to be achieved by continued efforts to be on the righteous path. Similarly an ignoble conduct is a product of continued actions in wrong direction.

Exercised by the virtues of thoughts, humans prefer to choose the right or the wrong path and subsequent guidance from God can bring contentment and happiness in one's life. Righteous thoughts and subsequent good deeds will bring rewards in lives of human beings.

So truthful thoughts can grow into perfection and messed up thoughts can grow into imperfection, people who remain in between these two types are the persons of varieties in degrees of deviation. In other words God can make a man to become the master of his own thoughts, character and destiny, thereby making himself what he wills.

QORAN advocates a man to find within himself the righteous deeds by application and analysis of its teachings. God watches, alters and controls a man's behavior and advises patience and perseveration in human thinking. Hence a man has to work to remove the wrong, useless and confusing thoughts and should cultivate pure and right thoughts to become a good director of his own life, as per the will of God.

The learning process is concluded by rewards out of wanted behavior and punishments out of unwanted behavior. Circumstances in life can influence a man's character, revealing to him how he should react to the circumstances, thereby becoming master of the circumstances themselves.

Mostly a man wants to have his destiny improved without trying to improve himself and instead he should acquire progress by making efforts in that direction, by trials, tactful measures, implementation of knowledge and wisdom. Indolent, deceptive and cheating behavior may get some benefit for some time but not all benefits for all times.

Curiously one does witness cases where disbelievers become rich and believers remain poor and resultantly feel suffering, but they should know that suffering has no standard criteria, as one man's suffering could be another man's routine, which means suffering is a product of negative thinking. One must also realize that blessedness is not possession of material things, but blessedness is TAQWA, which is being contended with what one has, so deprivation and poverty are not a burden. Affluence is only possible when a man builds himself to suit his circumstances and to use the circumstances as aids in progress.

Righteous thoughts usually shape into productive performances, which in turn make the circumstances congenial. Wrong thoughts or incompletely understood thoughts can cause confusing efforts leading to adverse circumstances. Then fear, doubt and indecisiveness can make a man weak and irresolute, which in turn can bring circumstances of failure. Similarly hatred and suspiciousness can cause accusations for others leading to conflicts, punishments and self-pitying for oneself, which can injure one's self confidence.

On the contrary righteous thoughts can bring grace and kindness, in turn invoking similar responses from others leading to cordial interpersonal relationships warranted for progress and harmony. As a man cannot choose his circumstances, but can choose to encourage correct thought process, it can modify his outlook towards his circumstances in a way to match his happiness. Eradication of wrong thoughts would also encourage the circumstances to provide him with opportunities.

Faith and belief in God controls fear, anxiety and depression, which would otherwise demoralize him to make him react differently to unfavorable situations. So total submission to God reflects peace and brings healthy thinking which can bring cheerfulness and energy, leading to happiness.

QORAN says a man's intentions should have a purpose, otherwise he may fall prey to worries, troubles, in turn leading to weakness and weakness cannot survive in untoward surroundings. The focus on religion should be just and true and the same focus has to be taken as duty with self-control and concentration for accomplishments, thereby helping a man to overcome his weaknesses leading to strength of character required for success.

It should also be known that strength can only develop from right efforts and practices in a consistent and continued fashion. Failures should be taken as tests from God for our learning so that we avoid committing the same mistakes again. Fears and apprehensions allow avoidance behavior, making the subsequent tasks even more difficult and there remains the possibility of continuously avoiding the same, which would lead to more fears, then fear of fears ultimately landing into a vicious cycle of failures.

QORAN advocated that oppression by and subservience to worldly authorities must be discouraged, one can understand this strategy that both the oppressing and the submissive/oppressed are in a way cooperating with each other out of ignorance. Hence a man is so designated that he is free to become either oppressor or oppressed by his own will and acts.

Exercising faith in God, following the teachings of the Prophets, following the path of right measures, struggles and sacrifices to live a life of calmness, adaptation, spiritual strength to increase a man's influence in society for permanent happiness, is the need of the time for believers. The 'Day of reckoning' is comparable to the last judgment accepted by Christians as the moment of truth, when the acts and deeds will be measured and every human being will be answerable for what it does. Even a tiny act of selfishness or an unconsidered act of generosity will be accounted for and the virtues of goodness would be rewarded.

The warnings about the Dooms day direct the believers to ponder over the implications of their behaviors on a daily basis. It marked the need for reminding the people who are prone to forget about the results of what they are doing. How it is important to cultivate the virtue of goodness and to refrain from selfishness, greed and arrogance. So also it registered the entire structure of cosmos, presence of other creatures, succession of day and night with regularity, the light and brightness of sun and moon, the shades of clouds and rains, all being the signs of God's control and existence.

If the mankind understands that they are completely dependent on God and the fate is already written for each, then there remains little scope for the mankind to feel for their own obligations and to own up responsibilities towards others, also they could feel undermined by destiny, a man will consider his frailty, and subdue his strengths. All which will be left would be humble thankfulness for what is given and destined for him.

QORAN cherishes a vision that guides us to the righteous path which reassures that even if uncongenial circumstances are present, they are not going to remain for long, as uncongenial environment itself provides time to develop latent powers and resources within ourselves and only then a man will look into opportunities for growth and contentment.

Muslims have traditionally expressed love and veneration for Mohamed. Stories of Mohamed's life, his intercession and of his miracles particularly "Splitting of Moon" have permeated popular Muslim thought. The QORAN refers to Mohamed as "a mercy to the worlds". Muslims experience Mohamed as a living reality, believing in his ongoing significance to human beings as well as animals and plants.

QORANIC recitations with the themes, words, phrases, sound patterns and the method of recitation with pauses and deep inhalations are comparable to breathing exercises of yoga. Certain verses and stories are repeated in QORAN for the purpose of emphasis. The rhetoric questions in the QORAN now also have modern day scientific explanation as having the benefit of imprinting the memory with the intended message. The questions like: Have you not heard? Do you consider or not? Have you not seen? In QORAN, verses followed by questions to bring awareness are now considered a recognized method of learning. But at several places the language of QORAN remained mysterious.

The QORAN has a powerful effect on all those who have read its words. One thing to note is that this is the *English translation of the directives of the QORAN.* The QORAN is in its original, pristine Arabic as it was revealed, so these verses as stand-alones may not be fully understood.

One must look into all the verses in relation to each other, the Sunnah and Ahadith, the context of revelation and scholarly understanding to fully interpret the QORAN's meaning.

However, it is highly encouraged for every Muslim to read the QORAN with best interests, preferably in it's original language Arabic, else hopefully this english translation or reflection will be a good starting point. "It is the duty of every Muslim - man, woman, or child - to read the QORAN and understand it according to his own capacity" as narrated by Prophet Mohamed.

All the characteristics of evil like treachery, lying, betrayal, lack of modesty, lack of awareness that God is always watching, lack of religious commitment, loss of piety, loss of chivalry and lack of protective considerations for others, this is like doing the opposite of what they are seeking. Whoever seeks the enjoyment and good things of life by means of that which God has forbidden, then God will punish him by letting him get the opposite of that which he is trying to achieve.

Hold strongly to Islamic principles, but remain adaptable to change when applying them in response to contemporary issues and challenges. Know Islamic history and civilization, and keep oneself intellectually equipped to understand Islam and issues of the world.

Be a good citizen, well adjusted for living in a secular state and multi-religion society, and contribute to global humanity. Appreciate the richness of other civilizations, be confident enough to interact with others and be prepared to learn from them. If God brings you to it, He will bring you through it.

The Islamic concept of God is that He loves, is merciful, and compassionate. But Islam also teaches that He is just and swift in punishment. Islam teaches a balance between fear and hope, protecting one from both complacency and despair. Muslims believe in the original unaltered Torah (the Gospel of Moses) and the original Bible (the Gospel of Jesus) as that they were revealed by God. However, none of those original scriptures are in existence today, in their entirety. Therefore, Muslims follow the subsequent, final, and preserved revelation of God, the Holy Qur'an.

Muslims believe in the law of personal responsibility. Islam teaches that each person is responsible for his or her own actions.

On the Day of Judgment Muslims believe that every person will be resurrected and will have to answer to God for every word, thought, and deed of theirs. Consequently, a practicing Muslim is always striving to be righteous.

Terrorism, unjustified violence, and the killing of innocent people are absolutely forbidden in Islam. Islam is a way of life that is meant to bring peace to a society, whether its people are Muslim or not. The extreme actions of those who claim to be Muslim may be, among other things, a result of their ignorance or uncontrolled anger. Tyrant rulers and those who commit acts of terrorism in the name of Islam are simply not following Islam. These people are individuals with their own views and political agendas. Fanatical Muslims are no representatives of the true Islamic teachings.

The word "JIHAD" does not actually mean "holy war". Instead, it means the inner struggle that one endures in trying to submit their will to the will of God. Some Muslims may say they are going for "JIHAD" when fighting a war to defend themselves or their fellow Muslims, but they only say this because they are conceding that it will be a tremendous struggle. But there are many other forms of JIHAD which are more relevant to the everyday life of a Muslim such as the daily struggles against self-desire, the struggle against a tyrant ruler or against the temptation of Satan, etc.

Women are not oppressed in Islam. Any Muslim man that oppresses a woman is not following true Islam. Islam grants Muslim women numerous rights inside the home and in society. Among them are the right to work and earn money, the right to financial support, the right to an education, the right to an inheritance, the right to being treated kindly, the right to vote and representation on a board, the right to receiving a dowry, the right to keep their maiden name, the right to worship in a mosque, etc.

TAWHID (the oneness of God) is the basic principle for Muslims upon which everything else, both religious and worldly affairs, is to be built; affirming that ALLAH is one. We see that the Jews and Christians differed concerning TAWHID. Allah singled his Apostles to perform miracles in order to establish proof against people. It is appropriate to say that EISA was a human being, whom Allah chose from among all of mankind to be created without a father, as a manifestation of the power of ALLAH to create a man outside the usual means.

The miracle of Adam's creation is greater. For 'EISA was created without a father, but Adam was created without a father or a mother, and this is more expressive of the power of ALLAH to create. In conclusion, the miracles which ALLAH gave to 'EISA were just like the miracles of all the other Prophets.

Of those Muslims who split up their religion i.e. who left the true Islamic Monotheism, and became sects, i.e. they invented new things in the religion (BI'DAH), and followed their vain desires, each sect rejoicing in that which is with it. ALLAH has commanded them to adhere to His Book and to follow the SUNNAH (way or path of His Prophet), as He says do not say or do anything that goes against the Book of ALLAH and the SUNNAH of His Messenger.

What is meant here is that Allah forbade the people to split into various groups, and He commanded them to be united, but they followed their own whims and desires, and they cast the Book of ALLAH behind their backs, and if they were confused about a verse from the Book of ALLAH, they did not refer to the Sunnah of the Messenger of ALLAH in order to understand it, rather they let their own opinion and corrupt reasoning be the judge.

It should be noted that God gave each Messenger his own laws and path. God enjoined TAWHID (belief in the Oneness of God) upon every single Prophet whom He sent, but the laws varied and some of them abrogated others. Some things that were permissible at the time of Adam were abrogated at the time of Noah.

The laws that existed at the time of Moses were partially abrogated at the time of Jesus, as God tells us that to each among you, we have prescribed a law and a clear way. So once this is understood, we will realize that plural marriage did not exist only in the law of Mohamed, rather it existed in the laws of all the previous Prophets. For example, Ya'qoob (Jacob) had two wives and was married to two sisters at the same time, according to the Old Testament, as it says in the Book of Genesis 29:15-35.

The QORAN is the last revelation to humanity and has been unchanged since it was sent down to Prophet Mohamed, in the 7th century. The QORAN's 114 SURAHS (Chapters) and 6236 AYAAH (Verses) are the source of every Muslim's faith and practice in the religion of Islam.

CHAPTER 3

Now comes the need to explore the validity of belief in one God, who is beyond doubt a very generous provider, as the availability of the consumables have never ended and does not seem to exhaust even in future, except until the dooms day. There comes the question of running the show and what to adopt for a peaceful living of the inmates of this universe. Which code of ethics is the best? Which ideology satisfies the universal flawless code to be true?

It is the human being alone, who is created in the best form in comparison to other creatures. The tact, the understanding, the capacity, the faculty, the strength and the intellect brings the human being to the privileged class among the living and keeps the non-living for the use and comfort of this privileged class. This is not a chance happening and not without an organized plan.

The provider of all the basic needs necessary for life is just one controller and there are ways and means of knowing the existence of the only controller. The dignity, honor and respect which are enjoyed by humans are not procured by chance again. The creations of galaxy, sun and moon, land and sea, earth and space do not benefit anybody except the mankind and this is enough proof of the supremacy which he enjoys over all other creatures.

We have to show abstinence from SHIRK (making partners to God) and is not expected out of us for all these favors given by almighty. Curiously it is a curse to rely on subjects, objects, authorities, contacts and means of influence and to form intercessors as it confabulates our expectancies and brings only temporary results, which even if gets clicked would lead to further dependence and would undermine one's coping resources and if it does not click, it would rebound frustration and so also would shatter our confidence levels defeating the effort itself.

The other responsibilities called FARAID (religious duties) are no favors returned to the almighty as they only benefit us and the society in which we live and are rather for our own good than for God so to speak. The enforced laws of religion actually attribute to our own peaceful living, in the best interests. But for that we have to follow only one constitution and it is possible if we submit ourselves to the belief in one God almighty, which has been revealed by God sent messages from time to time.

IMAN (Faith) is the most important pillar of any religion. In Islam it constitutes SHAHADAH (belief in oneness of ALLAH (God) and prophet Mohamed to be the messenger of God), SALAH (praying 5 times a day and thanking God for his blessings), SIYAM (fasting in the month of RAMADAN by testing one's endurance), giving ZAKAH (charity of 2 and half % of income and saved assets and allowing the deserving to share from the gifted ones) and performing HAJJ (pilgrimage to Mecca once in a lifetime and to care for others while living in unison).

Faith is belief in the righteousness and practicing it continuously. This continuity parallels the continuity of life and thereby brings effectiveness in manners, attitude and behavior. The basic faith in existence of God and the development of subsequent loyalty brings about the inspiration for good deeds, which in turn improvises the social relations.

Prayers with total submission to almighty makes one modest and humble, the same reminders of total submission for 5 times in a day keeps a man righteous in his deeds and helps excelling in his goodness.

Declaring the intention for prayers by heart or tongue focuses the initiation, intention and concentration and lastly to face QIBLA towards KABAH for direction [all believers face the same point of direction from all corners of the world for prayers], brings a universality among people of all nations.

The prerequisites for prayers are WUDHU (ablution) for cleanliness of the body and proper clothing for acceptability and grace of the society.

Partial 'Ablution' is cleaning of the exposed parts and orifices with water, bringing necessary hygiene and causing peripheral constriction of blood vessels to pool blood circulation to the center bringing clarity of thought and a sense of well-being.

Complete 'Ablution' is warranting a bath. 'Ablution' can be substituted with TAYAMMUM (dry ablution in absence of water) permissible in sickness, non-availability or harm by water, during travel, if there is fear of missing the funeral prayer or EID prayer.

Exemptions are granted for wearing socks on clean feet and on dressings over wounds of exposed parts, when wet hand can be passed over them to complete 'Ablution'. TAYAMMUM is undertaken by a universal method of lightly rubbing both hands on earth, sand, stone or walls and wiping over face, then right hand over left and left hand over right to highlight the initiation of prayers so as to mentally get prepared for its performance.

SALAH is an advantage to one who is following it, as prayers help one in achieving discipline, punctuality, thankfulness for God's blessings, which in turn divert us not to recreate ourselves in other's sorrows or to create self-gratification upon recreations. Religion helps us to cultivate the attitude of tolerance and to curb violence, terrorism, hatred towards other religions and faiths.

SALAH has to be performed on a regular and continuous manner just as nourishment has to be provided for survival on a regular and continuous basis and life had to lead on a regular and continuous healthy foundation. Prayers are not meant for pleasing God but they show an orderliness leading to a disciplined life for human beings, if they are undertaken on week days or weekends only or certain auspicious times, their purpose cannot be served.

Moreover God is not dependent on man for prayers, rather a man is dependent on prayers for his own good and in pursuance to the need for total submission to God, it brings about peace, harmony and happiness in a man's life. Other than prayers doing a lot of good, to a man, whatever good we do is for our own good.

The purpose of prayers is to prostrate and to extend thanks for unaccountable blessings given by God. One cannot extend thanks unless one is convinced of achievements provided by God and one commemorates contentment by extending thanks.

In a 24 hour cycle one spends life with a divisibility of 8 hours in work, 8 hours to rest and 8 hours for other social obligations and this cycle cannot be cut short or stretched further for fear of disruption of a balance, required for healthy living, so also one has to judiciously spend one's life with one third spent on acquiring worldly provisions, one third for relaxation and one third for performance of religious duties.

And by performing SALAH 5 times a day, one is reminded of the need to feel contended 5 times a day, which in turn is expected to bring the feeling of usefulness, happiness, reward and joy.

Prayers relieve humans of frustrations and depressions out of the tests we undertake or fail, but if they are done with total submission to God, it can bring calm, control and fulfillment in life as it will indicate the need for trials in the righteous ways and leaving the results to God, more so because a man cannot know what is good for him at a given time, later to realize that whatever happens, is for the good of it.

By reminding himself about the existence of God 5 times a day, and vocalizing QORANIC AYAAH (verses) is to interpret meaning of the same, a teaching warranted for a balanced living and also to strengthen his own belief, which will foster goodness in him in turn to reciprocate goodness in others, thereby creating healthy interpersonal relationships, much necessary for a harmonious society to reverberate peace in individual's life.

Prayers other than its physical steps of exercise to freshen up one's body and mind, are a sort of meditation to bring insight into one's capabilities and help relieving the brunt of stresses one can or cannot cope with. Prayers also constitute submitting oneself to God, to seek apologies for the mistakes, which will allow in becoming a good person and will disallow repetition of the same mistakes, very much required for success.

Prayers preferentially performed in congregation denote a sense of equality, belonging, unity and brotherhood, if done in its literal sense are equally important for a strong society, which can bring stability and in turn peace with a sense of security. Application of rules is necessarily put to prayers which are made obligatory for sane, mature adults free from sickness and exemption is given to women during menstruation and child birth.

Prayers or SALAH are classified as FARAD (obligatory), WAJIB and SUNNAH (supererogatory) and NAFIL (optional). They have strategically set timings to combine religion with worldly life and to remind a human being towards his duties to God. The timings have flexibility of execution, the protocol matches with the day and night routine, suiting the need to stretch as an exercise and to meditate according to present day medical science as follows:

1. SALATH UL FAJAR - (between dawn to sunrise)
2. SALATH UL ZUHR - (between noon to afternoon)
3. SALATH UL ASR - (between afternoon to sunset)
4. SALATH UL MAGHRIB - (between sunset to dusk and darkness)
5. SALATH UL ISHA - (between dusk to dawn)

Certain allowances are given for special prayers like SALATH UL QASR, which occurs when prayers of ZUHR and ASR plus MAGHRIB and ISHA can be combined to be performed as one and constrained in times of travel and sickness.

SALATH UL JUMA (which is the prayer of ZUHR of Fridays which is to be performed in congregation) with KHUTBAH (public preaching sermon comprising of praise to God), is like a convention which is recommended to ensure bondage, unity and solidarity among the brethren.

SALAH during travel are shortened to 2 units for all regular prayers and with 3 units for SALATH UL MAGHRIB, if travel is not extended to 2 weeks and distance traveled exceeds 48 miles, when WAJIB, WITR and NAFIL are forgiven. Prayers can be performed at a later time than the set schedule (ie delayed) for logical reasons and are termed QAZAH.

TAR AWEEH are prayers conducted in the month of RAMADAN after ISHA and comprises of 8-20 units. SALATH UL JANAZAH (Funeral prayers) are undertaken after regular prayers and 2 units completed in standing position.

Prayers are also performed during specific needs like during floods, draughts, eclipses, childbirth, marriage, before and after travel, in times of distress, upon visiting graveyard and as thanks giving after achievement, all coming under the category of NAFIL.

'IMAM', the leader of the congregation of prayers is chosen based on his piety and knowledge. Prayers in congregation favors 'no' class distinction, 'no' racial discrimination, 'no' color or creed favoritism and 'no' prejudicial partiality to anyone. All are considered equal in the religion, which curiously takes away pride if any and inferiority if any among the believers.

'EID' prayers are performed in larger congregation and at bigger scales, prayer of EID UL FITR marks the end of RAMADAN and prayer of EID UL ADHA marks completion of HAJJ. Distribution of alms and oblation is the major part of EID celebration. One must remember the deceased relatives and pray for their souls, to extend a hand of help to the needy, to show sympathy for the grieved and distressed, to visit sick people and to give words of consolation and to convey good wishes to all, with emphasis on give and take among the brethren, on the occasion of EIDs.

DUAS (invocations) are undertaken with sincerity and intention to seek forgiveness from God. Forgiveness is sought from others too, who are consciously or unconsciously hurt by one, because it becomes easy for the hurt to forgive others (against whom one lodges grievance) and in doing so interpersonal relationships are strengthened and community fosters harmony.

SIYAM is fasting with total abstinence from food, drinks, intercourse and smoking from dawn to dusk in the month of RAMADAN. Fasting is done with honesty and faithfulness to God only. It is a manifestation of total submission which teaches patience during deprivation, consideration of hunger for the deprived and cultivation of discipline out of self-restraint.

Fasting also invigorates control over physical temptations, increases will power, manages budgeting, economics, adaptability to change, accommodation during non-availability of essentials and lastly inculcates social belonging to a united community at large in which all are doing the same act at the same time across the globe, indicating a sense of equality, unity and brotherhood. Fast if broken by mistake is forgivable by God. TARAWIH, reading and understanding of QORAN, and social visits are recommended.

Medical science affirms the benefit of a light stomach, light body, light psychological and intellectual perceptions. Ramadan according to lunar calendar exposes the fasting to different geographical regions with different climatic conditions justifying the exposure to all types of adaptability. Fasting is also advocated for 3 days as alternative to breaking any promise or oath.

Fasting is a compulsion for all sane and able people over the age of puberty. Children, sick, insane, old or feeble people are exempted upon compensation of one full meal to any needy Muslim. Women in menstruation, pregnant women, lactating mothers and travelers are also exempted from fasting but need to compensate by making up for the lost fasts later at a suitable time. Willful negligence and breaking the fast without logical reason asks for a compensation of feeding 60 needy persons to discourage giving up or breaking the fast upon facing the strain of fasting, which again has to be observed at another day anyway.

Yet another obligatory principle is ZAKATH, which constitutes charity, alms giving, tax payment, voluntary contribution. This act is judged only by God and is actually distribution of one's share of annual income among the rightful beneficiaries. It signifies honesty with oneself without any governing body to check, but retaining the percentage of share is unlawful to God, as it signifies selfishness and greed, not approved by religion.

On the contrary ZAKATH motivates goodwill and good wishes for the contributor by equalizing the distinction of class plus induction of trust in the society. On the recipient's side, it reduces the suffering of the needy and a consolation to the less fortunate people. It creates a desire to earn more to distribute more and encourages the social responsibility towards community. It encompasses a balance between capitalism and socialism.

The math of ZAKATH is fixed at atleast 2.5% of annual income and assets lying with the possessor for a year's time. Worth of residential dwellings not included in the assets, unless they are put on trade, in which case the asset value becomes taxable and the amount given as loan is also taxable, as the returns are guaranteed wealth. ZAKATH is for net balance after deductions of all expenses. Cattle and agricultural products are also considered as assets. On non-availability of beneficiaries the amount can be deposited for future needs of the community in public treasury.

The recipients could be poor Muslims, needy relatives, new converts, muslin prisoners of war, indebted neighbors and workers employed for the purpose of collection of ZAKATH, Muslim scholars in service to God through study or research for the propagation of Islam, Muslim expatriates stranded in foreign lands, Muslim welfare organizations, deserving Muslim students for scholarship, orphanage homes and public service institutions doing good for the Muslim schools, Muslim Hostels and Muslim marriage centers. The contributor can use his own discretion for choosing who to give ZAKATH.

HAJJ pilgrimage to Mecca is obligatory at least once in the life time of a Muslim who is physically, mentally and financially capable to do it. Financial capacity means enough savings after expenses and liabilities towards the family. Debts should be paid off before initiation of HAJJ. It is the largest convention of believers visiting the house of God. It proves to be a test of endurance to keep peace with one another. It discourages aristocracy, royalty, and superiority and prejudices if any.

It is a tribute to the sacrifice of Abraham and Ishmael; one gets reminded of the history by repeating the ritual performed by Prophet Abraham. HAJAR al ASWAD, a black stone mounted during reconstruction of KABAH. The offering of sacrifice marks the end of HAJJ and abundance of flesh to be distributed to all Muslims all around the world who are less fortunate. The abundant meat is refrigerated, preserved, canned and transported either to other poor Muslim countries or the surplus can be sold and money used for charitable purposes. The sacrifice can be delayed to any convenient time or even place to serve the above purpose. The money for the sacrifice can also be used for any other noble legitimate cause.

Islam commands straight forward course of thought and deeds to best interest of all humans, but the western literature and some political agendas often confuse the world about the meaning of JIHAD as a terrorist act whereas it only means a struggle in the cause of religion more so in the personal lives where one is supposed to fight the evil temptations of the world and live a simple, peaceful life without causing harm to self and others. And world history denotes that the basic instincts of human nature not only muslims but people of all faith or no faith, has been that winning a war is a necessity for existence or power, but unfortunately muslims and Islam gets negative attention under this light.

It is true in relation to eradication of injustice, oppression, selfish ambitions and false claims. One has to fight against all these evils for peaceful survival of mankind and JIHAD is meant for the same. It is a fight against the evil.

Probably that explains the nature's necessity for wars taking place locally, regionally or globally. There were incidents that even victorious of wars were settling their gains or benefits by wars again. How could almighty not know the psyche of mankind and their actions in this regard and how almighty could have not mentioned these relevant human tendencies or traits with regards to existence, so ALLAH advocates JIHAD not on the misrepresented reasons but for a course of self-defense based on lawful and justifiable reasons, otherwise the earth would be full of mischief. ALLAH knows that there are people since times immemorial that had been waging wars or checking wars to disallow vested interests for power, easy money, and quest for assets to satisfy inflated egos.

PART II

BIOGRAPHY OF PROPHET MOHAMED

CHAPTER 4

The pre-Islamic era upheld the principle of two rival spirits of good and evil for a long time. Then the great religions of the world had spread the light of faith, but later they got changed in 'scriptures' and in their teachings. Christianity took the doctrine of Trinity, which are 'one God in three persons' father, son and Holy Ghost. Judaism the religion of Jews also had not remained firm in its belief in the unity of God.

Buddhism had been converted into an idolatrous faith. Later in the sixth century A.D., Hinduism went ahead of every other religion in the number of gods and goddesses. The Zoroastrians also followed suit in the hierarchy of gods and goddesses. All treated community of women as goods, which all men could enjoy and share, as they do air, water, fire and space. People used to offer prayers to the sun besides fire and water. Separate prayers were prescribed for rising and going to sleep, taking a bath, dressing, grooming, eating and drinking.

In the west around the same time rulers of, the Sasaniyan Empire were alienated from the people, as they regarded themselves as the descendants of celestial gods. The kings and nobles were enmeshed with massive wealth and treasures and were interested only in raising their own standard of living. The common people were, on the other hand left extremely poor and in great distress.

The result was that the peasants rose into revolt in many places, becoming bandits breaking into the houses of nobles to prey upon their property and to abduct their womenfolk. Gangsters took over the possession of landed properties and gradually the agricultural holdings became barren as the new owners knew nothing about the cultivation of land.

On the east, among the inhabitants of India there were outcasts and untouchables to ensure the superiority of the Brahmins. Its code of life was applicable to the entire society, dividing it into four distinct classes: the Brahmins or priests enjoying the monopoly of performing religious rites; The Kshatriyas or nobles and warriors supposedly governing the country; and The Vaisyas or merchants, controlling peasants and artisans; and the Sudras or the non Aryans were meant to serve the first three castes.

The social laws accorded the Brahmin class distinctive privileges and any tax could not be imposed on a Brahmin, nor could a Brahmin be executed for any crime. The widow should burn herself alive with the funeral fire of her dead husband. The Sudras, were the untouchables and could never acquire any property, nor could retain any assets and were not even permitted to read the sacred scriptures.

In Europe around the same time, the knowledge and all the literary and artistic achievements of the past were lost. The German races were raised to political power and they still debated the point whether a woman had the soul of a human being or of a beast. She could neither acquire nor inherit any property nor had the right to sell or transfer the same.

The Byzantine Empire was engrossed in the experience of its love for sports and recreation with moral corruption. Egyptian kingdom in that province was directed to the sole purpose of squeezing profits from the ruled peasants. Syria, another part of the Byzantine Empire used to treat the locals as slaves and kept them at their mercy.

The Greeks and the Iranians were peoples of a different type, accustomed to improving upon them and they lacked the morale to fight against injustice and brutality. No idea, no concept was attractive enough for them: no conviction or call was sufficiently proven in a way that they could jeopardize their comfort and pleasure. The common man of Byzantium and Persia with the conduct of the pre-Islamic people could see the difference between the social life styles of the Arabs and other nations of the world.

The continents of Asia, Africa and Europe, occupied the most suitable place for being chosen as the center of enlightenment for radiating divine guidance and knowledge to the entire world. All the three continents had been cradles of great civilizations and powerful empires, while Arabia lay in the center through which passed the merchandise of all the countries far and near, affording an opportunity to different nations and races for exchange of thoughts and ideas. Such a country, unimpeded by political and social constraints, was ideally suited to become the nucleus of a universal message preaching human equality, liberty and dignity.

The Arabs had been the followers of Abraham's religion in the olden times, which had the distinction of having the first House of God in their land.

In Arabia the idea of morals, was unknown to the ancient Bedouin, who were extremely fond of wine and gambling. The Bedouin maiden, enjoyed no social status, could be bartered away like other exchangeable goods or cattle or be inherited by the deceased's heir. A man could have as many wives as he liked and could dispose of his children if he had not enough means to provide for their sustenance.

The Bedouin was bound by unbreakable bonds of fidelity to his family, blood relations and, finally, to the tribe. Fights were his sport and murder a trifling affair. A minor incident sometimes gave rise to a long drawn warfare between two powerful tribes.

But In Arabia since ages Medina was an agricultural settlement, while Mecca was financial center. In those days only Taif and Medina were the places in Arabia which had water and grazing lands and Mecca was the place with barren lands and Rocky Mountains with no sustainable life. Tribal life was essential for survival and tribal grouping was encouraged by the need to act as a unit, this unity being based on the bond of kinship by blood.

There were too many people competing for too little sources, which led them to resort to aggression and violence and to wage wars for those resources. It had been a different struggle for existence and people used to practice invasion of neighboring territories in the hope of getting cattle and slaves, which was considered an acceptable method of survival. Native Arabs were constantly traveling from one place to another in search of water and pasture for their flocks, while the nomadic survival warranted raiding caravans, not viewing this as a crime. They only were bothered about remaining affiliated with tribes and believed in the tribal values, as people felt secured under the shelter of any tribe. As any tribe had to worry about the betterment of their own people and the practice of protection for the kith and kin of any tribe, they were expected to obey the head of the tribe. They had selfish motivations to do well to others in your good days so that they can receive the same from others in times of deprivations. The solidarity was restricted to the interests of individual tribes only.

In Arabia, gods or goddesses were considered as protectors of individual tribes and were associated with sacred trees, stones, springs and wells. Arabia was the site of an annual pilgrimage, at the 'KABAH' shrine, situated in Mecca which housed 360 idol statues of tribal patron deities.

Some native pre-Islamic Arab monotheists were also listed alongside Jews and Christians and Mohamed himself was a HANIF and one of the descendants of Ishmael, son of Abraham. But those people had little concern for God or any conventional religion or the existence of any supernatural power.

Mohamed thus belonged to the tribe of 'Quraysh', who were settled in Mecca for its miraculous water resource from 'ZAMZAM'. This tribe was inevitably dependent on trade, so they wanted eternal peace for the same and avoided tribal conflicts with others. Only this way they could allow segregation of merchants from distant places to do business in the times of Pilgrimage. Hence they forbid all kinds of violence within 20 km radius from 'KABAH' the holy shrine. Agreements were made among different tribe to disseminate attacks on mobile merchants and in turn they were paid to protect and guide 'CARAVANS'.

The season of pilgrimage used to bring richness to the inhabitants, who used to follow the ritual of 7 circumvolutions of 'KABAH', with its return to one point. All this pointing to the centrality of Mecca in the Arab world and the trade during pilgrimage times reinforcing self sufficiency of inhabitants.

CHAPTER 5

I n the year 570 Mohamed was born on the 12th day of RABI
AL AWAL (a lunar month) in Mecca, Saudi Arabia. The
clan of Mohamed 'BANI HASHIM' was very distinguished
among the tribe QURAISH and were also privileged for supplying
water to the pilgrims. Mohamed's father Abdallah having died
before his birth, his mother Amina was distressed, so Mohamed
was wet nursed by another lady named Halima and spent the first
6 years of his life, with her.

After his mother expired, his grandfather 'Abdal Muthalib'
reared him for another 2 years only before he also died. He then
came under the care of his uncle Abu Talib, the new leader of
Bani Hashim. Mohamed accompanied his uncle on trading
journeys to gain experience in the commercial trade. One of
his uncles Hamzah taught him archery and swordsmanship and
another uncle Abbas gave him the job of managing 'Caravans'.
Mohamed acquired the title of 'Al AMIN' meaning "faithful
and trustworthy" and was sought out as an impartial and reliable
arbitrator and grew up holding it.

At the age of 25 Mohamed was asked by a rich 40 years old lady,
Khadijah from another distinguished clan of 'Asad', to take a
Caravan to Syria. Khadijah was impressed by his competence
and honesty. She sent a proposal and Mohamed consented to the

marriage, which by all accounts was a happy one for another 25 years. Khadijah bore 6 children to Mohamed, among them his sons Al Qasim and Abdallah died in infancy and his 4 daughters namely Zaynab, Ruqayah, Um e kulsum and Fatima survived.

Later Mohamed's patron Abutalib got into financial trouble and had to give his 5 year old son Ali, in Mohamed's custody. Quraish were involved in Idol worship, whereas Jews of Medina and Khaiber retained their religion but intermarried with local people. But Christian communities in Yemen and Byzantium existed and Arabs kept contact with both Jews and Christians as 'AHLE KITAB. Christians believed that Arabs are the progeny of Ishmael, the oldest son of Abraham and they knew that both Abraham and Ishmael rebuilt the holy shrine of 'KABAH'. So every tribe came to Mecca to worship their own gods which were kept in the holy shrine.

Some of them were expecting that an Arab prophet is soon to arrive to bring the truth from ALLAH and would propagate the divine mission of revival of the religion of Abraham. Mohamed also knew these facts but did not realize that he is the chosen one to be given the prophet hood, so commonly known by the people of those times. They were also familiar with the belief that God is almighty who is identical with the God worshiped by Jews and Christians.

For that matter all the words of God from 'Zubur', 'Torah' and 'Bible' from times of Prophets David, Moses and Jesus who forecasted the arrival of one more and the last prophet from the sands of Arabia, was clearly documented in those books out of which some are known today and some not known. At some point Mohamed adopted the practice of meditating alone for several weeks every year in a cave of Mount Hira near Mecca. During one of his visits to Mount Hira, the angel Gabriel appeared to him in the year 610 and gave the first revelation from God. Mohamed was blessed with prophet hood on 'LAILA TUL QADAR' (the night of destiny) at his 40th year of life and QORAN was showered on him in succession.

Then he started telling about his revelations to his friends and family, who were willing to accept him as the long awaited Arab Prophet. Mohamed's wife Khadija was the first to believe he was a prophet. She was soon followed by Mohamed's ten- year-old cousin Ali, close friend Abu baker and adopted son Zaid, his daughters, 4 of his cousins and wives of his uncles, Abbas and Hamzah. Later Bilal also accepted the word of God and Mohamed to be His messenger.

Around 613, Mohamed began his public preaching, but most Meccans ignored him and mocked him, while a few others became his followers. There were three main groups of early converts to Islam: brothers and sons of merchants; the unprotected foreigners and the younger generation belonged to lower classes. Mostly they were women, servants and slaves. Mohamed kept retreating to get revelations and was asked by the angel to listen to the revelations completely, without attempting haste and was instructed not to try understanding them prematurely until the full significance is made clear.

The words of those revelations were first recited by Mohamed and later chanted and memorized by skilled literates and preserved by scholars, who wrote them. The same message which initially Mohamed preached a selected few was ordained to preach to the whole clan of 'Bani Hashim'. So he invited 40 elders for a meal, which was frugal and meager indicating absence of lavishness and unwanted hospitability. They were made to understand that luxury is waste of money and squandering. Prophet then addressed the gathering notifying the revelations. The invitees were reluctant to accept his words.

Mohamed continued his preaching and people resented to accept. People thought that he may have the ambitions for monarchy, in spite of knowing that Prophet is not supposed to aspire for any public office control and should remain a messenger only. Quraish disappointed Mohamed, because of this antagonistic behavior. He went back to the elders of the clan and explained the misunderstanding and corrected them that Islam is not the same religion which was followed earlier. He taught the principle of 'TAWHID' (oneness of God) which signifies that all are equal and that all must take ALLAH as one God, without partners.

The Quraish forced Abutalid, prophet's uncle to abandon him, so that they could kill him. But Abutalib did not cast him out and remained Prophet's patron. Abulahab was the half brother of Abutalib and opposed Prophet's message, and who had also given 2 of his sons in marriage with 2 of Mohamed's daughters, Ruqayyah and Um kulsum, asked his sons to reject their women, which they did. Then Uthman ibn affas offered to marry Ruqayah and he did.

By that time Quraish leaders of opposition discarded Mohamed's prophet hood. So the time of 'JAHILIYAH' continued but revelations urged Mohamed to remain calm, forbearing, patient, gentle and courteous. The opposition in Mecca became stronger when Mohamed delivered verses that condemned idol worship. As the number of followers increased, he became a threat to the local tribes and the rulers of the city, whose wealth rested upon the KABAH, the focal point of Meccan religious life.

Then Quraish started persecutions and ill-treatments of Mohamed and his followers including the weaker Muslims and slaves. The situation started becoming so grave that Mohamed sent the vulnerable Muslims to Abyssinia, where a Christian Governor gave them asylum. Then Umer ibn al Khatab got converted to Islam which created a big blow to the other Quraish clans. Mohamed expressed God's word that there is no force or compulsion to accept Islam and still all can live in peace.

In the year 619 Khadijah and Abutalid expired, making Abu lahab as the chief of the clan, who was an ingrained enemy of Mohamed, denied the clan's protection for Mohamed, which placed him in danger. Afterwards Quraysh started torturing Mohamed in different ways along with Abubakar, who wanted to join immigrant community in Abyssinia. Another chief of clan by name Ibn Dugmuah gave protection to Abubakar and allowed him to stay back in Mecca. But Abubakar was not allowed to recite QORAN or pray in public.

Mohamed then visited Taif, another important city in Arabia, and tried to find a protector for himself there, but his effort failed and further brought him into physical danger. Mohamed was forced to return to Mecca. Mohamed was brought under the protection of another chief of clan, namely 'Nawfal'. He continued preaching Islam but the people remained hostile towards him.

Once while Mohamed was resting in one oasis and while he was reciting QORAN, a group of strangers presumably Jews overheard him and were impressed and according to 'TORAH' they canvassed that another prophet from Arabia has come after Moses. A delegation consisting of the representatives of the twelve important clans of Medina, invited Mohamed as a neutral outsider to Medina to serve as chief arbitrator for the entire community. The delegation from Medina pledged themselves and their fellow-citizens to accept Mohamed into their community and to physically protect him as one of themselves.

During one of the pilgrimages Mohamed preached and some people of Medina accepted and approved his message and considered him as the last messenger, as was told to Jews. So initially 6 pilgrims accepted Islam and volunteered to invite other tribes to this religion. While these developments were taking place Mohamed married the sister-in law of one of the chiefs of clan by name Amir. She was a widow and named 'Sawdah', who was 55 years old and took hold of Mohamed's household.

In the next pilgrimage the 6 converts brought 7 more and they assembled in 'Aqabah' and pledged to worship ALLAH and to accept Prophet's social justice. Then one trusted Muslim by name 'Musab ibn umayr' accompanied these people to Medina and preached others, who started getting converted to Islam. Now Mohamed and his followers planned to migrate to Medina, but they had to abandon their homes and had to seek protection from strangers.

Mohamed instructed his followers to migrate to Medina until virtually all his followers left Mecca. Being alarmed at the departure of Muslims, according to the tradition, the Meccans plotted to assassinate Mohamed but he secretly slipped away from the town with Abu Bakr. Mohamed was to shift in the end but by that time his protector chief died and the other chiefs of Quraysh planned to kill him. Mohamed and Abubakar hid themselves in a cave, at the entrance of which spiders weaved webs and a dove laid eggs and sat in the nest. For the searching parties it was impossible to assume that any human could have entered the cave and hiding inside.

The Muslims of Medina were anxiously waiting for Prophet to join. After 3 days of hiding Prophet and his aide Abubakar moved towards Medina taking a circuitous route. They stayed for 3 days in Qubah on the way and then reached Medina, in 622.

The emigrants were called 'MOHAJIREEN' and the hosts were called 'ANSAR' (Helpers). The Muslims of the Medina wanted Mohamed to stay with hem and begged him for the same. Mohamed could not show any favoritism so he let his mare to lead him to his place of stay under the guidance of ALLAH.

The mare sat at a place meant for drying dates, which belonged to one Ansar. Prophet negotiated to purchase that portion of land and allowed construction of a mosque which later became the place for public and political meetings. He permitted Christians and Jews also to worship in the same mosque, considering them as part of God's family. The mosque was completed within 7 months of HIJRAH (emmigration to Medinah) and in one of the walls a stone marked the direction to pray, 'QIBLAH', which was Jerusalem at that time. 'AZAN' was introduced to call the believers for prayers 5 times a day.

Among the first things Mohamed did in order to settle down the longstanding grievances among the tribes of Medina was drafting a document known as the Constitution, "establishing a kind of alliance or federation" among the eight Medina tribes and Muslim emigrants from Mecca, which specified the rights and duties of all citizens and the relationship of the different communities in Medina, including that of Muslims. The community defined known as UMMAH (brotherhood in faith) with a religious outlook was also shaped by practical considerations and substantially preserved the legal forms of the old Arab tribes. It formed the first Islamic state.

Following the emigration, the Meccans seized the properties of the Muslim emigrants in Mecca. Economically uprooted and with no available profession, the Muslim migrants turned to raiding Meccan caravans as an act of war, deliberately initiating armed conflict between the Muslims and Meccans. Mohamed delivered

QORANIC verses permitting the Muslims to fight the Meccans, while muslim families emmigrated to Medina in small groups and ANSAR gave them shelter.

In the same year, Mohamed made the expedition of Tabuk towards northern Arabia because of their hostile attitude adopted against Muslims. Although Mohamed did not make contact with hostile forces at Tabuk, he received the submission of some local chiefs of the region. A year after the Battle of Tabuk, the local tribe, sent emissaries to surrender to Mohamed and adopt Islam.

However, the bedouins maintained their independence and their ancestral traditions. Mohamed then made a military and political agreement with them to acknowledge the sovereignty of Medina, to refrain from attack on the Muslims and their allies and to pay the ZAKAT tax (the Muslim religious levy).

Prophet having introduced a system of 'Brothering', in which meccan emigrants were made brothers to ANSARS and brought the practical concept of 'UMMAH', a common community. Then Mohamed brought the reforms based on ALLAH's directives conveying faith, prayers, sharing of wealth, concern for the community, the principle of forgiveness and to make peace with other non-believers.

In the end of 623 Mohamed received another revelation to turn the direction of QIBLA towards Mecca instead of Jerusalem and during his prayers he made the congregation, to face the house 'KABAH' built by Abraham as QIBLA, to make believe that Muslims are not following any footsteps of older faiths. Prophet Mohamed received a revelation that God allows people to attack to defend themselves and protect from hostilities and the message was pluralistic again, advocating protection of mosques as well as churches and synagogues.

The Battle of Badr began in 624. Though outnumbered more than three to one, the Muslims won the battle. Seventy prisoners had been acquired, many of whom were ransomed in return for wealth or freed. Mohamed and his followers saw in the victory a confirmation of their faith. The victory strengthened Mohamed's position in Medina and dispelled earlier doubts among his followers. As a result the opposition to him became less vocal. Mohamed expelled one of three main Jewish tribes from Medina. Following the Battle of Badr, Mohamed also made mutual-aid alliances with a number of Bedouin tribes to protect his community from attacks.

The attack at Badr committed Mohamed to war with Meccans, who were now anxious to avenge their defeat. To maintain their economic prosperity, the Meccans needed to restore their prestige, which had been lost at Badr. Muslims after the battle of Badr made treaty with Jews, for not to side the Meccan Quraiysh and in return were granted religious freedom. Some of the wealthiest Jewish tribes rebelled and after a siege of 2 weeks they were forced to surrender. Instead of punishment prophet gave them clemency. One of the prisoner of war, Abu Al Aas was freed without ransom, on condition that he would return his wife Zainab (Mohamed's daughter) and their daughter Umaimah to Medina.

Since Abujahl was killed in the battle and Abu lahab also died shortly thereafter, Abu sufian became the chief of Quraiysh. After the battle prophet's daughter Ruqayyah died and Uthman was grieved, so he was given prophet's another daughter Umm kulthum in marriage. Prophet's younger daughter Fatima got married to Ali and they were blessed with 2 sons Hasan and Hussain.

Prophet married 17 years old Ayesha, daughter of Abubakar with whom he lived till his 56th year of age. He married another widow, daughter of Umar, Hafsah. The other wives were Safiyah a Jew convert and Zainab was the daughter of the king of Abyssinia, where Muslims were given refuge and protection. Zaynab was the divorced wife of his freed Negro slave Zaid and adopted son. Then Juwairiah was married to prophet, and this led to freedom of many families enslaved.

All these subsequent marriages took place between his 57th to 60th years and were contracted mostly for political, social or humanitarian reasons, these wives being either widows of Muslims who had been killed in the battles and had been left without a protector, or belonging to important families or clans whom it was necessary to honor and strengthen alliances.

Mohamed did his own household chores and helped with housework, such as preparing food, sewing clothes and repairing shoes. Mohamed is also said to have had accustomed his wives to dialogue; he listened to their advice, and he allowed the wives to debate and even argue with him. He always considered them equal and gave liberty as companions. He even used to carry his wives on military expeditions, which gave women a new dimensional access to politics.

Abu Sufiyan subsequently gathered an army of three thousand men and set out for an attack on Medina. The next morning, at the Muslim conference of war, there was dispute over how best to repel the Meccans. Mohamed and many senior figures suggested that it would be safer to fight within Medina and take advantage of its heavily fortified strongholds. Younger Muslims argued that the Meccans will be huddled in the strongholds and would destroy Muslim prestige. Mohamed eventually conceded to the wishes of the latter, and readied the Muslim force for battle.

Thus, Mohamed led his force outside to the mountain of Uhud (where the Meccans had camped) and fought the battle of Uhud. Although the Muslim army had the best of the early encounters, indiscipline on the part of strategically placed archers led to Muslim defeat, with 75 Muslims killed including Hamza, Mohamed's uncle and one of the best known warrior. The Muslims buried the dead, and returned to Medina that evening. Mohamed subsequently delivered Qur'anic verses which indicated that their defeat was partly a punishment for disobedience and partly a test for steadfastness.

The Meccans did not pursue the Muslims further, but marched back to Mecca declaring victory. They were not entirely successful, however, as they had failed to achieve their aim of completely destroying the Muslims. Abu Sufyan now directed his efforts towards another attack on Medina. He attracted the support of nomadic tribes to the north and east of Medina.

Mohamed's policy was now to prevent alliances against him as much as he could. Whenever alliances of tribesmen against Medina were formed, he sent out an expedition to break them up. When Mohamed heard of men massing with hostile intentions against Medina, he reacted with severity. Around a year later, Mohamed expelled the Bani Nadir from Medina.

In 626 Zainab died only after 8 months of her marriage and Prophet Mohamed married another widow, Hind/Umm salamah, sister of another chief tan of Mecca, with 4 dependent children at the age of 60 years of age. She became the spokesperson of the women of Medina. Mohamed also married Maimunah, sister-in-law of Abbas, his long time ally.

With the help of the exiled Bani Nadir, the Quraysh military leader Abu Sufiyan had mustered a force of 10,000 men. Mohamed had about 3000 men, but adopted a new form of defense unknown in Arabia at that time: the Muslims dug trenches wherever Medina lay open to cavalry attack. The siege of Medina began in 627 and lasted for two weeks. Abu Sufyan's troops were unprepared for the fortifications they were confronted with, and after an ineffectual siege lasting several weeks, the coalition decided to go home.

During the battle, the Jewish tribe of Qurayza, located at the south of Medina, had entered into negotiations with Meccan forces to revolt against Mohamed. After the coalition's retreat, the Muslims accused the Bani Qurayza of treachery and besieged them in their forts for 25 days. The Bani Qurayza eventually surrendered and all the men, apart from a few were converted to Islam. Thereafter other Jewish tribes continued to live in Medina, keeping friendly terms with Muslims.

The victory over the battle of trench greatly enhanced the prestige of Muslims in the peninsula and prophet was also aiming at the termination of Jahiliya, so he had to address his message in another way, other than strikes-counterstrikes and atrocities against retaliations. In the siege of Medina, the Meccans exerted their utmost strength towards the destruction of the Muslim community. Their failure resulted in a significant loss of prestige. In the mean time Prophet Mohamed married Juwayriah, daughter of one another chief of clan and sealed another alliance with her father.

Although Mohamed had already delivered QORANIC verses commanding the HAJJ, the Muslims had not performed it due to the enmity of the Quraysh. In 628 Mohamed was directed from God to make HAJJ pilgrimage. He was not supposed to carry any weapons, but Muslims were reluctant to go into enemy territory without arms. Mohamed ordered his followers to obtain sacrificial animals and to make preparations for a pilgrimage to

Mecca. Then about a thousand volunteers joined and went to the border and stayed there for permission of entry.

Quraiysh resented and disallowed the pilgrims to perform HAJJ, so Muslims could not visit KABAH and only sacrificed their animals and shaved their heads, a ritual without going to MINA, ARAFATH and MUSDALFA (Obligatory places of visit during HAJJ), and Prophet signed a treaty to return back and not to wage any more sieges on Meccan caravans, in turn publicizing gentleness, non-violence and Islamic ideals and permission for pilgrimage next year. Since then the strength of Muslims grew many folds, resultant to the strategy manifested in treaty of the HUDAYBIY YAH (Important historical event in Islam).

Negotiations commenced with emissaries going to and from Mecca and a treaty, scheduled to last ten years was eventually signed between the Muslims and Quraysh. The main points of the treaty included the cessation of hostilities; the deferral of Mohamed's pilgrimage to the following year; and an agreement to send back any Meccan who had gone to Medina without the permission of their protector. Many Muslims were not satisfied with the terms of the treaty. Prophet diverted Muslims to Khyber, from where Jews were exiled but asked for peace and another agreement of peace was negotiated. Situation in Arabia improved and prophet called back the Muslims in Abyssinia and also married Ramalah, the daughter of Abu Sufian the chief of Quraiysh as another political move.

In 629 Prophet led another pilgrimage to Mecca and 2600 pilgrims performed lesser HAJJ, which is permission of entry to Haram, without visiting Arafath, Musdalfa and Mina. Muslims retreated back as per the agreement and showed their fair intention, which allowed expansion of converts and considered a big political triumph.

However, the Qur'anic chapter AL FATAH (The Victory) assured the Muslims that the expedition from which they were now returning must be considered a victorious one. It was only later that Mohamed's followers realized the benefit behind this treaty. These benefits included the inducing of the Meccans to recognize Mohamed as an equal; a cessation of military activity posing well for the future; and gaining the admiration of Meccans who were impressed by the incorporation of the pilgrimage rituals. In the same year Mohamed freed a Jewish noble woman Safiyah and married her, but his daughter Zaynab died.

In 630 Prophet Mohamed sent a large force from medina for conquest of Mecca and achieved a big victory without blood shed, thereafter Abu Sufian and Hind accepted Islam and their children were given important public offices. Then came another success in the battle of Hunayn, occupied by the tribe of Hawazin, who accepted Islam and other important people of Quraiysh accepted Islam. Prophet reinstated the Quraiysh officials on their posts and old time enemies were given promotions and Gifts. He declared an amnesty for past offences and some of these were later pardoned. Most Meccans converted to Islam, Muslim opposition was almost removed and Prophet's work was complete after 10 years of HIJRA.

In 632 at the end of the tenth year after the migration to Medina, Mohamed carried through his first truly Islamic pilgrimage, thereby teaching his followers the rites of the annual Pilgrimage (HAJJ). Mohamed delivered a famous speech, in which he advised his followers not to follow certain pre-Islamic customs and to align the lunar calendar. Mohamed abolished all old disputes and old pledges, as prerequisites for the creation of the new Islamic community.

A few months after the farewell pilgrimage, Mohamed fell ill and died on the 12 day of Rabi ul awwal 632, in Medina, at the age of 63. He is buried where he died, which was in Aisha's house and his grave now housed within the Masjid e nabwi, in the city of Medina.

CHAPTER 6

A fter his death came the era of four KHALIFS (successors) who continued the prophets mission of preaching of QORAN for generations to come. QORAN is the God sent word through revelation given to Prophet Mohamed, the messenger of God and historians and Muslim scholars attempted reconstruction of the life of Prophet as honestly and a truthfully as they can.

During the time of Prophet Mohamed, the QORAN was mainly preserved through memorization. Hundreds of Companions of Prophet were HUFFAZ, or memorizers of the whole QORAN and QORAN was also preserved through writing. Prophet Mohamed made special arrangements to have it written down. When Prophet Mohamed used to receive a revelation, he dictated it to a Companion, who wrote it down on anything that was available: bark, stone, bones, leaves, etc.

The companion then read, what he had written, to the Prophet. If there were any mistakes, Prophet Mohamed would correct it and then let it be brought before everyone. Prophet Mohamed also told the order of the verses, etc. and they were written accordingly. So, in the days of the Prophet one copy of the QORAN existed of what he had gotten written under his personal supervision. It was not in book form but in different parchments. Other Companions also had collections of the QORAN for their personal record but no standard copy of the QORAN in book form existed.

After Prophet Mohamed died, Abu Bakr became the first Khalifah (caliph), who foresighted the need of the compilation of the whole QORAN in the form of a Book. In the battle of Yamamah and other battles, many HUFFAZ were martyred. Umar noticed this and went to the Khalifah, and told him about this matter. Abu Bakr seeing the importance of this agreed. Then Zayd bin Thabit who used to write the QORAN for the Prophet during his time was called.

The compilation of the QORAN started. Lots of companions, including him had memorized the whole QORAN and so the QORAN could have easily been written down from memory. There were also complete collections of the verses of the Holy QORAN available with many companions. Zayd bin Thabit used both methods by collecting verses that were written during the time of Prophet Mohamed.

Verified the verses, with his own memory, seconded by Umar, testified by witnesses, collated from companions and compared for documentation.

The purpose of this transcription was to prepare an organized document so that reference could be made to it when required. The transcripts stayed with Abu Bakr. After his death in 634 CE they were passed on to the second Khalifah Umar. And after Umar they were given to his daughter, Hafsah. When Uthman became Khalifah in 644 CE, Islam had spread to far areas.

After having these standard transcripts prepared, all other copies of the QORAN became uniform in script and the sequence of Surahs, leaving no room for differences. The copy produced by Uthman is still extant. All copies of the QORAN available today in the world are exactly identical to the Uthmani Version, which was completed less than twenty years after the death of Prophet Mohamed. It is the word of God revealed to the Prophet Mohamed, over a period of 23 years (from 610 to 633 CE). The QORAN is still in its original form as it was revealed to Prophet Mohamed.

Later some improvements were made in the Arabic script, like the adding of dots, punctuations and diacritical marks, to make it easier for non-Arabs to read, but of course, the text of the QORAN has remained, and will remain the same forever. God sent QORAN bestowed mankind with a mission to create an honest and decent society, where all the members are treated equally with respect and in turn mankind has to surrender completely to God, which is the meaning of Islam.

Within hundred years of the demise of Prophet they started collecting his sayings known as 'AHADITH' and his practices in life known as 'SUNNAH'. They are considered a model of emulation for pious Muslims and has to a great degree influenced the Muslim culture. The Sunnah also played a major role in the development of the Islamic sciences. It contributed much to the development of Islamic law, particularly from the end of the first Islamic century.

PART III

QORANIC DIRECTIVES

CHAPTER 7

In the name of ALLAH, the Beneficent, the Merciful

Praise be to God, Lord of the Worlds, The Beneficent, the Merciful, Owner of the Day of Judgment, you (alone) we worship ; you alone we ask for help, Show us the straight path, The path of those whom you had favored ; Not (the path) of those who earn your anger nor of those who went astray.

Believe in God, who created you and believe in his holy book and his messenger who guides you to the right path and in the Day of Judgment.

Perform all kinds of good deeds. Believe in unseen, pray and give alms from the funds given to you from the almighty.

Do not lie or riot on the land you live. Do not cheat or follow the stray and the unadvised that are in darkness. Keep relationships intact, but keep distance from those who severe and break ties.

Do not make partners to God, even like undue reliance on authorities and exaggerated dependence on material pleasures, which concurrently deprives you of self support structures leading to nothing but frustrations.

Those who trust the religion subsequently would be profited by its teachings to seek peace of mind and in turn will get the rewards of convenience, comfort and happiness.

Human nature with its errors of thinking, pitfalls of understanding and shortcomings of wisdom try to displace their misgivings by unhealthy competitions, unwise judgments and uncalled for prejudices.

Those who try to seek solace by hypocrisy are actually inviting losses to themselves. You are put to test according to the guidance provided and are allowed to choose the correct path.

Prayers may be a difficult ritual but definitely not for those who are dedicated and obedient.

You are given supremacy over other species and races, but you are not supposed to abuse these privileges and instead you should remain steadfast.

If you continue committing mistakes, ask for forgiveness and God will forgive you, in the hope of seeing your gratefulness.

The minimum you could do is by repaying thanks for God's obligations, but by denying the same you do not hurt anybody, instead you harm yourself.

Never cross the boundaries, as it is the limitations which harmonize self and the society. And do not forget that in spite of your deviant actions and abstinence from keeping to your promises, God kept showering blessings and sympathies on you.

You should learn from your past experiences and historical events which have bearings in themselves and lessons for the future.

Do not attempt pretense in attitude and try fooling around with others.

Worship no one except the one God; treat well your parents, relatives, orphans and the poor. Speak softly and good of others, pray in unison and give charity to the deserving.

Do not assault one another and do not displace others from their houses.

You are given clear instruction about good and bad deeds, right or wrong path. Understand the tests involved in life.

Hesitate to indulge in bringing conflicts among married couples, which is no less a sin. You are invited to think, analyze, weigh and scrutinize before performing an act. All the credits you will earn in the good cause will debit prize.

Ignorant are those who have drifted from their right path and still ask for the signs as proof to get convinced about the eternal.

God gives the worldly amenities desired by some. Prophets were sent among themselves, who could reach, preach and teach them to improvise their lives. You are answerable for your acts, and people before you for theirs.

Disbelievers will continue criticizing your actions; you don't have to get afraid of them. You fear God as it would keep you away from sins. The reward would be the path of righteousness for your own good.

Patience is the ultimate requirement for peace of mind and contentment in life.

There will be times when you will be tested by dangers, harassments, hunger and pain, loses of lives and property, downfall from normalcy in economy and securities.

Endurance, patience and tolerance are needed to not only win against basic struggle in life, but to earn ultimate and eternal solace and privileges.

Even acts of goodness should be enacted by your earnest wish and will, and not done by any subdued pressure.

In spite of clear presentations denoting examples of signs of God being the creator, moderator and controller, those who defy the fact of God's eternity and greatness would also be forgiven, conditional to their ratification, and rectification of their wrong doings.

Except for those who were allowed lifetimes to correct themselves, and if they do not do so and die without belief, they will not be pardoned; neither will be allowed another chance, as there is a limit of concessions.

Otherwise the perseverance in unwanted behavior may become persistent, repetitive and devoid of repentance.

God has created the skies and the Earth, and the galaxies and the universe, as a permanent platform. See how the movements of stars and planets are in fixed orbits from which they do not deviate.

The transportation in sea is made possible by the density of water and its specific gravity and the clouds are carried by winds necessary to sprinkle the rain at specific places on scheduled timings.

The plantations grow from seeds with water showered by rains and different creatures are born with attributes suitable for their geographical habitat. See that there is no other alternative for these destined and organized setups and do not refute these factual proofs.

You are permitted to relish HALAL and to refrain from HARAM and pork. You should also avoid eating any things which is forbidden except if you are innocent about it or cannot help otherwise, without intending to cross limitations.

It is not sufficient to perform rituals to seek advantages from God. A true believer believes in one God, the doomsday, existence of angels, QORAN as the God sent book, and the prophets.

Your assets and money that you cherish are to be spent on the needs of your relatives, orphans, deserving, needy and paupers and in freeing the slaves.

True following is organizing SALAH and giving ZAKAT. Righteous are those who keep to their words and are patient in times of stress and difficulties and in tests of discriminating the true and false.

At your terminal times, for your assets and properties, you should leave wills in popular methodology for your kith and kin. This is your righteous choice. In case one realizes that intentionally or unintentionally he is deprived of his rights, then he could present his case in front of elders and well-wishers.

Fast in the month of RAMADAN as was instructed to earlier races, for your own good, which would also increase your tolerance thresholds and capacity for contentment. If you have failed to do so, on some reasonable pretext the same should be performed at other times in similar counts.

Those who are eligible for fasting and had not done so should give FIDYA which is feeding one deserving person against loss of one fast. It would be more good and rewarding, if you extend more in lieu of prescribed compensation. But remember that it is better still, if you keep your fasts obediently, except those in journey or sickness, who could fast the missed numbers equally at other times.

Call for your needs only to God and pray for your wishes. God will listen and grant, whatever is asked for, conditional to true belief in seeking and getting help.

God grants company of your wives during the month of Ramadan, other than the fasting time. Your spouses will cover your weakness and you do the same for them.

But God has set certain restrictions for the enjoyment of companionship during ITIKAF in the mosque and has also set a pattern of preferences for worship and hope, so do not exploit His directives.

Do not infringe on each other's belongings and money, and do not bribe your authorities to get permission for corruption. Advocate openness and avoidance of dishonesty in life. Do not get carried away by cults and omens and get rid of orthodox and false beliefs about right or wrong.

If you are being oppressed because of your faith, you are permitted to fight, but do not go into the extremes as God does not allow extremism. Fight for your rights for cunningness must be curbed.

Perseverance is required to tackle oppression, so persevere to eliminate the root cause.

Practice the principle of balance, but do not exceed the limitation imposed on you and keep to boundaries. Give alms as per the teachings of QORAN and never antagonize your own values and virtues. Do not get into difficulties by own misdeeds. Try to be good and obliging to others.

Make intention to perform HAJJ or UMRAH and attempt doing so. In case you fail in undertaking the task, do not avoid giving sacrifice of animals, which is bonded on you.

Except for those of you who cannot give sacrifice, you have been given the relaxation of fasting for 10 days, 3 days during HAJJ and 7 days after reaching home. During performance of HAJJ it is obligatory on you to refrain from misconduct, wrong deeds and quarrels. During the journey to HAJJ carry all necessary things and practice patience and inhibitions. You can also earn your living during the performance of HAJJ.

Those who preferred the ways of denial are also sanctioned certain privileges in life as that of luxury and pleasure, which may test your patience and restraint, but you will be placed higher in the end.

There were people who believed in extremism and selfishness, in spite of teachings of goodness, and prophets being sent to them to guide them towards the right answers to their problems.

You are not being tested as your predecessors were tested with hardships, endurance and difficulties until they cried for help, which was provided to them with grace and promise.

As regards to drinking alcohol and gambling, both are forbidden, as they are evils which may appear to provide some relaxation or petty benefit, but the sins will outweigh their benefits.

Spend the extra money over and above your needs and requirements among the deserving. As regards to the question of orphans, do what is good for them. You are encouraged to share your amenities with them.

With regards to menstruation, keep away from physical contact during those times and resume normal relations after that. Wives are like farms for you and you may go to them to avail the best out of them.

Those who take oath to detach themselves from their wives, preferably should rejoin within 4 months. However, if they intended divorce, womenfolk who are only once or twice formally divorced must remain tolerant for 3 menstrual periods and not hide conception, since these may be grounds for resumption.

Women also are privileged with the same position as men, they have equal rights over men and men have equal rights over them, but men are relatively given more authority.

After 2 TALAQS either woman should be accepted or separated with honor and respect. Give whatever are the rights of wives and never consider recovering the already gifted amenities. Except if woman is asking QULA and wants separation after certain compensations or compromises.

After third TALAQ, the wife will become HARAM, unless she marries another man and seeks another TALAQ. Then if they feel they can follow the norms of the religion judiciously, they can get remarried. Do not harass and hurt their feelings by holding them in disharmony, it would be considered oppression and the person doing so will suffer its own wretchedness.

About the conceived child, if wishful the mother should feed the child for 2 years, during which time husband should give alimony. Do not exceed the restrictions upon each other. Do not press wives for more and do not put husbands into distress.

Such decision about feeding mother's milk should be on mutual agreement.

Alternative could be to use surrogate mothers for breast feeding upon a reasonable compensation.

Widows may lay low for 4 months and 10 days (IDDAT), after which they may lead their life as they wish. Regarding the intention to marry a widow, stay tolerant till they complete IDDAT and express wishes in the most accepted terms.

TALAQ could be given without conjugation, but the payment of half the MAHR is abiding on you, more for rich and less for poor. It is preferable that women do not demand MAHR, in which case, if men can afford it they should pay in full. Each one should consider and compromise for each other. In mutual transaction, try to be good to each other.

Cultivate and organize SALAH, especially the middle ones and devote yourself to the almighty in SALAH and present yourself with obedience and respect. In circumstances like stress or journey, perform shortened SALAH as directed to you.

Write wills in favor of the descendent wife, for one year alimony, food and shelter for one year, unless they wish to leave the house on their own will and pleasure. Similarly, a divorced woman should be awarded her rights, as it is duty of honorable people.

All prophets were given grades of supremacy. Moses was awarded conversation with God and Jesus was privileged by eternal powers of healing and rejuvenation.

Be generous with your assets and earnings, spend as per the directives. Distribute ZAKAT among the needy, as this richness is also given to you by God, as it will be returned back in several folds.

Softspokenness and hiding other's mistakes to avoid humiliation to them is even better than giving alms. Never extend financial assistance to make them feel weakened. It would be like a charlatan who publicizes his charity for fame and satisfaction of his ego.

You would be like a blessing and fruitful plantation which is destroyed by a calamity, while you are old and you still have children who are weak and are dependent on you. It warrants some serious thought and analysis of your position.

Do not keep the best and give the worst to others. Imagine a situation in which you are treated similarly, then how you would feel and react. Only those who are intellectuals can understand these lessons.

It is permissible to give charity openly but if you keep secrecy in such matters, it is even more commendable. Rather by doing so, you are seeking pardon from many more evils.

What you spend in the good cause is only doing well to yourself. You should be doing this in its true meaning and rest assured that you will never be deprived of the rewards.

Especially deserving charity are people who have devoted themselves in the service to God and do not find time to earn their living. People do not understand their suffering as these people do not express their needs or ask for help and assistance openly. And if you help and support them, it will be registered in the good books of God.

You may be warned that taking interest on money is forbidden. Unknowingly whatever advantage you have taken out of ignorance about taking interest taking, that would remain between you and God, but if that it is highlighted, then refrain from continuing to do so, otherwise hell will become your destiny and you will remain there for ever. Forbade the interest on money liable on others and undertake repentance at least now, so that you get back your into righteous investments.

Do not oppress others and you will not be oppressed. If you have given loan to a person, be patient in recovery, if the taker is tight handed and it will be much better if you waive off the liability on analyzing the truth. It is preferable if you are lending money as loan, put it in writing. Keep a trustee to record the terms. The literates should not refuse such a request to make such a document and allow the receiver to pronounce in words so that he should abide by it for fear of God and stick to the conditions spelled out.

If the taker is illiterate, his representatives should do the same in the equal justice. Then take two witnesses from male acquaintances. If they are not around take one male witness and two female witnesses, for one may remind the other. Witness should be such that both the parties hold faith in them. And witnesses should not refuse such a service if called upon even if the matter is small or big.

On reaching agreement in time, do not neglect recording the facts at the earliest.

This is the beneficial system as you will not get into doubts about deals. Though not compulsory, it is recommended that in regular business dealings, keep a witness while undertaking transactions. Also abstain from putting the trustee or the witness into inconvenience, otherwise you will be put to proclaim the sin.

If you are traveling while transacting such matters and you do not find a trustee, deal with honesty but avoid fraud and return the mortgage with honesty. And never hide the facts you have witnessed, as it is a sinful act.

God only puts the amount of burden on you that you have the capacity to shoulder. Good deeds will have good returns and bad deeds will have bad returns.

QORAN contains guidance with clarity in certain scriptures, and some scriptures have subdued meanings which human intelligence cannot decipher.

The desired objects and subjects are loved and wanted, which is a known weakness of human beings, like womenfolk, children, treasures and wealth, means of transport and yielding land.

There is temporary relief in worldly comforts, but in the end you have to stay with the destined fates. The best are the comforts and amenities of Heaven and God's favors. The good ones are those who are patient, who speak the truth, who are obedient, who spend to please God and who ask for forgiveness.

God appoints rulers and dethrones them. God gives fame or defamation on his own discretion and showers his blessings on whom He wishes. God created life from innate things and controls the seasons.

You should remain righteous as all good and bad deeds will be uncovered one day. Every prophet and his family are all members of a single community. God chooses anyone who deserves. The example is of Jesus. He gave the prophet the power to heal grave diseases and the power to put life into the dead.

God-sent books have an advisory value and God-sent messages have a purpose of their own. QORAN is the last testament of God. Jews and Christians claim inheritance from Abraham. Their holy books were sent to them after him. Abraham was neither a Jew nor a Christian. He was a Muslim who believed in God.

Return trustee's worth, honor your word, refrain from malpractice, never try to claim other's property and do not break your promises, otherwise you will be made to suffer on the Day of Judgment.

Prophet Jesus never claimed himself to be God, he passed on God's word for people to follow. None is equal to God. Muslims should believe in Prophets sent before Prophet Mohamed too, for God does not discriminate among his prophets.

Do not bring rift among yourselves, because God has brought you closer when you were living in the stress. Work to preach the right and you will be forgiven of your sins. Forbid fellow human beings from wrong ways and guide them the right ways.

Advise directed at you is meant to keep you from harm's way. Make acquaintance with the righteous and do not care for the astray. Remain steadfast in times of ease and stress; those who control their anger and are forgiving are the loved ones of God.

If you commit wrong, ask for forgiveness from God, as it is the first step towards correction. You will not remain lazy or depressed and if you a true believer, total submission to God is a way to desist temptation of avoidance and gloom due to worldly events.

You are put to test at certain times to know who are patient and who will remain steadfast in the cause of religion. God blesses those who are obliged to him. Those who want worldly pleasures are awarded the same and those who are apologetic and perseverant are awarded both worldly comforts and the eternal joy.

Do not repent on the losses and do not mourn on death of loved ones, everything is God gifted and it is not your own, to perceive its loss or separation.

Believe in destined fates. Every person dies at a predefined hour. Believe on the Almighty, as it is only after total belief that you can get the solace required for a harmonious living.

Be happy with whatever is showered on you and avoid comparison with others, as you are not aware of who would be contended in the end. Those of you who are contended are better than those who are trying to achieve more and are awaiting contentment. Greed and wishful thinking disallows the satisfaction and there is no criterion of the norms for satisfaction.

Do not attempt treason with fellow human beings as you would be answerable for the same. Try spelling the truth about your thoughts.

In times of war and defeat the intention of God always remain clear to distinguish between true believers and those who say they believe but in their hearts do not. You may be asked to bear the painful and if you prove patient and pious, you will be declared brave. Meet the commitments and regard your words.

The creation of earth and the space and the cycle of day and night, in themselves are signs for the intelligent, as they are not meant without any purpose.

God does not deny the fruits of one's labor. Work is always rewarded, more so work in the cause of religion.

Do not seek favors in the name of God and do not break relationships within the family, clan and society. God will protect your interests. Remain considerate towards the orphans and do not acquire their assets by mixing with yours.

You are allowed to marry four wives but if you cannot do justice with all, you will have to restrict to only one. Give alimony to your wives and MAHR due for them, unless they give some exemptions, in which case you can avail the privilege.

Do not handover your funds to unintelligent, especially which is meant for your survival. It is better to give them amenities from it and treat them with kindness.

Be a guardian to the orphans, teach them the tact of living, and on finding them to have become mature, return their belongings in the presence of witnesses.

Men and women hold their righteous share from the property of their elders and parents. At the time of the divisibility of such shares consider the relatives and the needy that also deserve some and give them some of it and speak politely to them. Do not forget that you may be placed in a similar situation when you would leave children, who if ignored would cause a lot of grief, so be logical and reasonable in your transactions.

One part of share for the male is equivalent to two parts of share for the female. In case if there are only female heirs and more than two then each would get their share. If only one female heir is left then she would get half of it and the parents of the deceased would get one each, one sixth of the share. If the deceased did not have children then their parents would get one third of the share and in case the deceased had many brothers then the mother would get one sixth of the share.

All this divisibility of shares would be valid over the left over property, after the execution of the will of the deceased and after the payment of his debts. In case the wife leave their property upon death and they do not have any children then you would get half and if they have children then one fourth of their share, from the left over of their property after execution of their will and payment of their debts.

Similarly your wife would get one fourth if you do not have children and if you have children then they would get one eighth of the share, from the left over of the property after execution of the will and payment of debts. These shares are designated by God and would remain final, as he only is knowledgeable and wise.

If they are without parents and children and have a brother and a sister, then they will get one sixth of the share and in case the siblings are more than two then all would have to share from one third, from the left over after execution of the will and payment of the debts, conditional to no one else is put to loss.

God approves pardon for those who commit sin unknowingly and forbade from repeating and seek repentance, but not for those who continue committing sins and continue repeating them until terminal times and then seek repentance and desire pardon.

It is not permissible that you become heir of womenfolk and retain them to get some benefit out of your past giving. Only if they commit shameful acts then you may retreat from them in a polite manner. If you decide to marry another woman and even if you have given a few treasures out of treasures, refrain from collecting anything from it.

Avoid getting into marital relationships with the women who were married to your fathers as it may cause prejudices and problems. It is forbidden to have physical relationships with mothers, daughters, sisters, sisters of your father and sisters of your mother, so also women who have nursed you, your half-sisters, mother-in-laws, daughter-in-laws, sisters of your wife and the girls who remained under your guardianship and wives of other men. These are orders which are binding on you. You could marry women outside these relations conditional to their consent, payment of MAHR and in keeping of sanctity of marriage.

Profit yourself with rightful means, indulge in just business and refrain from committing suicide. Do not commit bigger sins like SHIRK, defaulting rights of parents and telling lies. God will forgive your petty sins.

You deserve the value of what you have earned. Do not crave for more, except asking God's favor, as he is the master of the universe. Only the genuine heirs will get their ancestral shares. You should meet your commitments and extend what is agreed upon, as God is there to watch.

If you anticipate disharmony and conflict among couples then select a just representative from both the sides and if they advocate compromise then they must adopt the good path of union.

Behave kindly with parents, relatives, orphans, poor, neighbors, servants and companions, as God disapproves pride and boastfulness. Do not practice misery otherwise God will stop the blessings and will subject torment. Those of you who do show off, adopting a pretentious behavior, and do not believe in God and the Day of Judgment, they are doing evil and only siding the devil.

Any sincere good deed will be rewarded doubly. Do not go nearer to SALATH while you are under the effect of liquor, until you can understand the meaning of your own expressions. Refrain from praying after mating unless you bath and get clean, except if you are traveling. If you are sick and cannot find water for ablution, then put your hands on clean soil and wave on your face, as God is forgiving.

There are some who speak high of themselves and boast, but they are mistaken. There are a few who lodge jealousy against those who are blessed by God's mercy. It remains God's wish to bless a few and deny others.

Those who deny the words of God they will be punished severely in fire, until their skins are burned and revived and burned again in Hell. Those who would believe and do good deeds they will be sent to Heaven where they will be awarded with streams, shades, comfort and wives.

In case of disputes leave the verdict to God and His messenger, as wrong and evil decisions will keep you stray. Keep distance from hypocrites, but continue to show them the righteous path, but at their level of understanding.

Whatever decisions are taken by the Prophet and reported by him have to be accepted with obedience and whole heartedly. If hypocrites are ordained to leave their home and sacrifice in the path of ALLAH, very few will agree to it, but if they do, they will be rewarded.

Obedience to God and His messenger is righteousness of high order.

For the directives which you do not understand seek guidance from wise men, who could guide you in the best interests and would disallow your confusion to effect others. Continue your struggle in the path of God and continue encouraging good deeds of believers to let them get re-enforcement to continue the same. The good deeds you recommend also derive some reward for you and vice versa.

Repay blessings by blessings, as every deed of yours will be recorded and will be audited on the day of resurrection. Do not surpass actions which you cannot control.

Make treaties with people who are tired of aggression or warfare and are extending compromises.

Any believer can not kill another believer, unless committed by mistake, in which case compensate by freeing a slave or pay due consideration for the victim's blood to his heirs. It would be different if they are willing to forgive you. If the victim is a Muslim and belongs to your opponent group, then only freeing a slave or equivalent is compulsory.

If the victim belongs to a camp with which you are exchanging treaties, contracts or dealing with them, then both freeing a slave and compensating by paying a consideration for the blood becomes liable. Incapacity or incompatibility to do the same warrants fasting for 2 months and seeking forgiveness from God. If someone does kill a Muslim on intention, then the verdict from God is Hell, where he had to remain facing God's wreath.

Oh, believers undertake research before enacting any deed in the way of God.

If someone extends the blessing of SALAAM (Peace be on you), even if he is not a believer and do not deny and comment that he is not a believer.

Those of you who have remained weak and oppressed will be questioned by the angels before they die as to why they did not emigrate and performed their duties and will be sent to Hell. Exceptions are helpless men and women and children who did not get the righteous guidance may be forgiven.

Those of you who would leave their homes for the sake of God and follow His prophet will get better places and wider homes.

While traveling you could shorten the prayers (SALAT UL QASR) and if confronted by enemies then perform prayers in groups covering each other with arms, so that you remain on defense and disallow disbelievers to attack you. But if there is no threat then perform prayers as usual on usual timings.

You have been bestowed by the book of QORAN, so that you decide your path according to the principles with which God has familiarized you. Do not side with those who disrupt the role of a trustee. Never fight for the causes of disrupters of trust, as they may hide facts from others but can not do the same from God, moreover you may only take sides in the world but can not do the same on the day of resurrection.

Those who do evil deeds and sins should ask pardon from only God, as only He can forgive or empathize, because the sinners have to bear the burden of their sins. Those who commit sin and then blame other person for the same have done open and graver sin and would face the brunt of it.

God has given you the QORAN and has tutored you with things which you were not aware of, which is God's blessing on you. Seek advice from those who are pious and say and do well for the sake of God. Those who resent Prophets and QORANIC teachings will face Hell only. God never pardons one who partnered Him, which is the biggest sin. All other sins can be forgiven except this.

Any woman who is afraid of harshness and negligence from her husband can decide her own path and both can agree on certain terms of gracious separation as it is not a sin. It is not possible from you to do justice with multiple wives, so do not neglect your duties and directives and correct yourself if you are doing wrong and remain contended with what you already have.

If a husband and wife are divorced then God will not keep them dependent on each other anymore, rather they will be made indifferent from each other and would become discreet towards each other.

Oh! believers stick to justice for the sake of God, become true witnesses and give true evidence, even if it is going against you, your parents, relatives, loved ones or even if it concerns a rich man or a poor man, do not get carried away by selfish motives and do not leave the balance in justice.

If you take side of a liar or if you lie, remember that God knows everything. MUNAFIQEEN are those who would continue showing faith and continue to deny it repeatedly and they will loose God's guidance and would face a torturous punishment.

Do not keep company of those who ridicule QORANIC verses, otherwise you may become one like them and may face the wrath of Hell. MUNAFIQEEN try to play tricks with God, by superficially remembering and pretending to pray, but they are misguided and cannot seek the righteous path, so believers should keep their distance have faith in God.

As they will ultimately land in Hell, unless they correct themselves, ask for forgiveness, develop faith and practice Islamic principles, only then they will be with believers and would get rewards.

God dislikes encouraging bad and evil deeds and also dislikes publicizing such deeds, except if you are oppressed and you intend to raise your voice against them. God also does not approve of incomplete faith, by believing in some Prophets and not in others, so do not differentiate between the prophets of God, otherwise punishment will be imminent.

Moses' followers argued with him, applied to witnessing God in person and worshipped the Calf but they were punished accordingly. The people upon whom Jesus was sent brought disgrace to Mary's chastity, claimed to have crucified Jesus, but they were confused as God replaced Jesus with a lookalike before the crucifixion, and lifted Jesus to the skies.

Revelations were sent to prophets. He gave the book ZUBUR to David. God had named some prophets and did not mention some others. God had spoken to Moses in person. He sent Prophets for all races for their own good.

God addresses the AHL AL KITAB that Jesus' birth was His wish and verdict for Virgin Mary. God does not need a child. Jesus was a chosen Man, who did not refute his role, neither felt pride nor had grandiosity and God sent a certification on that account, to let people understand and accept him as a messenger.

Regarding inheritance from a dead man with no male heirs and only a sister, the sister would get half of his assets. If there are two sisters, then they will get one third each. Among Heirs of the inheritance, males will get twice the share of females.

Oh! Believers keep up to your commitments. You have been allowed permission to eat herbivorous animals and not those explicitly prohibited. If you are in IHRAM you may not hunt. Do not neglect the verses of QORAN and do not neglect the months declared sacred. Never hunt animals that are meant for sacrifice, or that belonging to someone.

In deeds of goodness and righteousness keep supporting one another. You are forbidden from eating animals you found dead, blood, pork and those animals which are not slaughtered in the name of God. Those animals that have been suffocated or suffered injury or casualty by fall or attacked by other carnivorous animals but are still alive may be slaughtered and eaten.

Muslims are allowed to eat animals slaughtered by AHL AL KITAB. Women of AHL AL KITAB can be married after payment of MAHR, provided they believe in Unity of God and are pious.

Ablution is mandatory before prayers, and taking bath after mating, unless you are traveling or are sick or if water is not available then TAYAMMUM is the alternative. All this is to see that the routine life is not made difficult. This is to make you feel pure and for you to enjoy the blessings of God, so that you remain thankful.

Be judicious while bearing witness and do not get influenced by personal prejudices against anyone, as justice is equivalent to worship. Those who have broken their promises and forgot the guidance have dejected the trust and would be cursed, but not all are the same. So you may forgive them and continue obliging them, as God likes those who forgive and obliges others.

Those of them from AHL AL KITAAB who considered Jesus as the son of God have become non-believers. The last prophet was also sent to them to enlighten their faith.

Do not follow the example of those who have become party to crime including Murder and become losers. If you kill one person in God's eye it's like you have killed all of humanity, and if you save one person it's like you have saved the entire humanity.

On the day of judgment, your assets won't save you from any due punishment.

If those who listen to lies or practice forbidden things come to you for justice on their conflicts, you may either neglect them, or pass a sentence judiciously.

Do not neglect the God's advice for petty benefits. The followers of Torah and Bible have deviated from the God's message. Stick to QORAN, which accepts the previous books. Prophet was advised to deal with issues in the light of QORAN.

If God intended, all the followers of different religions would have been made one, but God wished to test you with the teachings of

QORAN. Do not come under their influence. If they turn astray it was intended by God.

Whoever from Muslims, Jews, Christians or those who believe in Astronomy and Astrology have faith in God and the day of reckoning, and do good deeds, can remain fearless and without despair.

Jesus, son of Mary was a messenger of God and not God himself. His mother was a steadfast lady. They both had to eat to survive and these were the signs for the thinkers.

Oh! Believers do not oppose things which are permitted for you, and do not cross limits. Swearing oaths, if done habitually and without purpose is meaningless, but swearing to misguide and cheat others will not be forgiven. If you swear to reinforce your commitment, you should respect your word and execute it. If you fail to do so you will have to feed 10 deserving humans and gift clothes to the needy, or free a slave or fast for 3 days. This is to rectify your mistakes and ratify your intentions.

Oh! Believers, drinking liquor, gambling, and fortunetelling are evils. Remain far away from them as they will begin to create differences, conflicts and hatred among you and may come in way of your prayers, so remain cautious. Faith, good deeds and TAQWA are positive characteristics liked by God.

God has permitted sea food without prefixed restrictions, which is a blessing you should remember well.

God can be strict or kind. God knows everything. There are certain things which are kept hidden by God on intention, so refrain from further enquiry into the same. Certain things which are not disclosed could as well be annoying to you.

God does not approve of believers to seek other resources for help, other than God Himself, but nonbelievers continue doing it and they are not intelligent.

Blindly following traditions is not right, as forefathers may not have been perfect.

Oh! Believers make will, with two witnesses from wise and pious men. If you are traveling or have fallen sick, those two witnesses should take oaths publicly to remain impartial and truthful, even if they are related to the beneficiaries.

Even prophets will be inquired about the eventualities, to which they will not be able to answer, they being humans themselves and are not aware of God's strategies. Jesus will be asked to recall, having been given the power to vocalize in infancy, given Prophecy in adulthood, books as a blessings, the power to imbibe life, to heal the blind and the lepers, and to revive the dead by God's will, which nonbelievers labelled as magic.

Jesus will be reminded of the people's wish to get 'Heavenly Meal' to get convinced of his prophecy, and Jesus requested God to send food from above, and God accepted it, with a warning that if they do not believe they will be punished severely.

CHAPTER 8

All human beings are made of mud or dust, which constitutes all the basic elements. Death is destined and fixed and so also the day of reckoning.

God knows secret thoughts, and hidden feelings among the obvious attitudes and the apparent behaviors humans do routinely.

God had been kind and He had compelled Himself to be so, but on the doomsday losers will remain losers.

The blessed will not be punished on doomsday.

Be familiar with Prophet, as you would be familiar with your sons.

Sinners have to bear the burden of their own misdeeds.

Don't you understand that the world is a transient place of comforts, but the life thereafter is for pious people?

QORAN addresses the Prophet that his unhappiness is justified as the people have not just denied him but denied the God sent message. Prophets sent earlier underwent similar circumstances but they remained patient until God's help rescued them.

God points out the limitations of Prophets, they being human beings, who could neither build a tunnel in the earth nor erect a ladder into the skies or perform a miracle on their own.

If God wished all would have found the righteous path, do not become one among the unintelligent. Only those find guidance that give attention to it. The dead will be brought back to life and will return back to God.

They insist on exhibition of portents which God alone could send, but they are ignorant of signs. Races earlier to Prophet's time were also tested by sickness and poverty so that they express humility and modesty in their attitudes.

God tests people by allowances of provisions, which may make them, feel proud, but they may be disappointed in the end.

God sent messengers as bearers of good news. Those who develop faith will not remain apprehensive or depressed and those without faith will be punished on that account alone.

QORAN advocates that Prophet is not blessed with any treasures neither he has any knowledge of the unseen. He performs his duty of conveying God's message.

Those who are on the right path and seek God's countenance will be protected. God had prescribed for Himself mercy for human beings. He is best of the deciders and has knowledge of unknown. No leaf is dried without his intent and no grain is sown where it cannot grow and nothing gets lost. All is noted in the clear record.

God induces sleep in the night and awakens you to allow the term appointed for you to accomplish your lifespan. He will proclaim what you used to do.

God appoints caretakers upon the deserving and He is omnipotent towards his followers. God is swift and who else can establish rescue from the claws of perils of earth and water, He relieves people from stresses and despair. No intercessor is there to replace Him.

God creates rebellion from subordinates, cruelty from the rulers, formulates confusion among yourselves, and creates enmity within yourselves to make you taste the tyranny of one another, all being punishments from God. God teaches guidelines by all pretexts so that people understand the meanings.

Everything is destined at a time and disclosed at a given time. Keep away from those who are carefree and playful with the matters of religion, and also those who are misdirected by their own doctrines without directives of QORAN, as people ultimately fall prey to their own characteristics. They are those who perish by their own.

Those who have lost their way must guidance, and surrender completely to the Lord of the worlds. God is the almighty creator of the lands and skies, controller of the doomsday and knower of the hidden. His is the sovereign Leader of the day when the trumpet is blown.

It is worthy of mentioning that the father of Ibrahim, Azar was a disbeliever and considered his progeny to be misdirected, but God had shown Ibrahim the creatures of the land and skies to strengthening his faith.

Disclaim worshipping the stars and the sun, as all set at some time and are under control of the God. God raises degrees of wisdom for the chosen ones and elevates esteem of those He chooses.

God selected the chosen few as his prophets and their children, parents and brothers are given dignity and position. God's words are guidance to all through His scriptures and commandments. The book of TORAH was revealed to Moses with clear principles.

QORAN admits the previously sent words of God, so that the people in and around the mother of villages are cautioned. God has the power to bring life from death and death from life.

God create cleavage of the day break and appointed nights for stillness and kept orbits for sun and the moon to function, brought light from stars as direction in the darkness on land and seas. Beyond doubt these are revelations open for those who have knowledge.

God showered rains and grew plantations out of it, created food in the form of cereals and dates as fruits in the low and far, spring pendant bunches and gardens of grapes and olive plants and pomegranates which ripen to give nutrition are all clear signs and portents from God.

You worship God and God will keep balance of maintenance for life. He is aware. Signs are extended for the intelligent to follow the truth.

Do not degrade or vocalize obscenities against other faiths and their gods and followers of other religions as they may do the same against you, your protectors and God.

God had sent His book with glad tidings and open teachings, the chapters are clearly educative and nobody can change the context of the Book.

Most of the people of the world may misguide you as they live with presumptive knowledge and deny the truth. You are given allowances, refrain from eating the forbidden unless you are pressed to do so on some genuine needs. There are people who default without any grounds and are led astray by their own lust through ignorance.

Avoid outward and inward sins, as sinners are made to commit crimes and to live in distorted concepts, but they are actually fooling themselves and plotting against themselves and are not aware that they will ultimately be punished.

Those who are on righteous path will be given wider tolerance threshold and those who follow evil path will remain narrow minded and impatient. God enforces one aggressive personality over the other and allow bifurcation in groups out of their misdeeds. Each of you will be assessed according to individual merits and rewarded accordingly.

There are some who discriminate and cross limits, even slaying their own children. They have indeed gone astray. Your assets are for proper utilization and you are blessed by crops of different plantations and fruits with different tastes like or unlike, to share among the deserving. Do not become prodigal.

Those misguided set forth a method for others to follow, so remain righteous and oppose offers which are forbidden for you.

Do not form intercessors to God, take care of your parents, do not neglect your children or dependents, even in times of deprivations. Shameful behaviors should not done either openly or secretly. Do not grab the shares of the weak or orphans and remain their trustees till they attain the age of maturity.

Keep justice in weights and measures and do good to others and you will be rewarded manifolds. You are made viceroys on the earth over the helpless and God has exalted some of you in ranks for the sake of testing, as God is swift in persecution.

God would inquire the messengers and the people for whom messengers were sent regarding the outcome of their efforts. QORAN narrates the events of origin of the world, when God made Adam from clay and ordained the angels to bow down to him.

Only IBLIS resented on the contention that he is superior over the human being, because angels were made out of fire. On this disclaimer of IBLIS, being proud was asked to leave the skies, but on his request to give him respite for time till doomsday it was sanctioned. IBLIS claimed to misguide the human race and challenged to be tested till then.

Adam and Eve were allowed a place in the Heaven with freedom but were cautioned to refrain from going near a particular tree. IBLIS misguided them and by deceit brought them near the tree, and they tasted the fruit from it. As a result of this they were shied and their shame became manifested to them and they desperately attempted to hide themselves. God reminded them of His caution and they repented upon their act and asked for forgiveness, so God sentenced them to be sent down to the earth for a time bound period where they were to live and die and be resurrected.

God addressed the race of Adam that they are bestowed with dresses for themselves to decorate their bodies as well as to be adornment and this is a sign in itself. People were told to remain modest with their garments and apparel and waste not in excess. The race of Adam were again cautioned to be on guard with SHAITAN, who succeeded in expulsion of Adam and Eve from Heaven. God made the evil ones friends to those without faith. Those of them while doing evil acts and shameless actions disdained it to be traditional. God forbade all shameful acts done openly or secretly.

God pointed out as to how people could partner the Almighty and form intercessors to God when there is no proof of it. Do not label God's name on things. Everything is time bound and destined and when time comes everything will be restricted and they can not advance it or delay it.

Oh! Children of Adam, messengers will be sent amongst you to pass on my orders. Those of you who follow them will be rescued from apprehensions and lurking sense of injury. God does not expect things from you which you are not capable of undertaking.

God will remove hostilities and indifference from entrants of Heaven, with a peaceful life there on, but each one will get what one deserves. Each one will be identified by their face value. The inhabitants of Heaven will neither be afraid nor be unhappy.

Do not get carried away from others as no one has authority, unless willed by God. Messengers were sent with glad tidings. Universe was formed in six epochs of time, galaxy was fixed, days and nights were separated and follow each other in a system with fixed orbits of Sun, Moon and other planets under God's order.

Pray to God in silence and with severity and God does not approve of those who cross the limits. Make sure footing with your Lord. World is modeled to live so do not create havoc and disorder in it. God sanctioned kindness for the righteous people.

God created undercurrent breezes which carry clouds on dry lands to shower rains to cultivate it for production. Similarly on the day of resurrection the dead will be raised. The land which is fertile will produce good plantations and the land which is less fertile will bring less production.

God had sent the verses of QORAN for those who are wise enough to understand them and remain thankful. QORAN described the events of Prophets Noah, Hud, Saleh, Lut and Shoeb who carried glad tidings but the people disobeyed them and were punished by natural calamities.

God guides people to perform weights and measures with correction and not to create mischief in the world which is set in order. Most of the people are not obedient and rebellious.

Prophet Moses was sent to the people of Egypt but the leaders questioned his authenticity and took his miracles as magic. They brought sorcerers to show magic but Moses stopped their falsehood which they faked.

The Pharoah was then provoked to take revenge who ordered to slay the male children and to leave the female children for slavery. God punished the Pharoah's race by bringing years of drought, shortness of crops to receive admonition but the race remained astray then God brought calamities and diseases both endemic and epidemic.

Weak and oppressed were made inheritors of east and west and God showed blessings on them. God's blessings were showered on Bani Israel for their forbearing, endurance, patience and consistency and God dismantled the infra structure created by Pharoah.

God gave Moses 40 nights for communion and Moses handed over the responsibility of preaching to Prophet Haroon (Aoron) and to continue the mission and instructed him not to follow the undisciplined.

Moses appeared before God on the scheduled time and asked for God's reflection. He forewarned him regarding his inability to envision God. God sent then thunderbolt which devastated the mountain (KOH E TUR) and Moses lost his consciousness. Upon recovery Moses admitted his shortcoming and confessed his faith. God extended Prophesy on him which he was asked to accept and to remain grateful.

God encrypted certain commandments on tablets on all matters and gave them to Moses for guidance and teaching. God expressed the desire to keep away the ordinances from those who feel pride and who even after witnessing the signs will not accept faith and will follow the evil path, because they denied the God sent word and remained ignorant.

Those who deny God's word and did not believe in the day of reckoning will be found lost and will be punished. The people of Moses started worshiping a calf decorated with jewelry, which was an injustice in itself.

Then the people asked for forgiveness. Prophet Moses was unhappy and grieved and informed his people that they committed a blunder. In anguish he caught his brother Prophet Haroon, who said that his trials went in vain so not to ridicule him and not to include him in the misguided.

Moses requested forgiveness from God for himself, his brother and sought His blessings. Moses collected 70 people for a destined time, who were subjected to violent quaking and died. It was a test from God. God gives guidance to the selected few.

Moses sought God's willingness for pardon and blessings in the world and the world thereafter. God punishes those whom He wishes but extends his mercy on all other things. God promised mercy on those who fear Him, give Zakath and believe in God's signs.

Those would seek ultimate reward only if they believe in unlettered prophets mentioned in their own scriptures, preach the righteous principles, and discriminate between HALAAL and HARAAM. A section of the people of Moses accepted to do justice in the light of truth. God bifurcated 12 tribes among themselves and Moses was asked to hit a stone with his staff and 12 streams started flowing out of it and every one found their source of water and God placed clouds upon them and sanctioned MAN O SALWA to relish food for them and to remain in humility but disbelievers brought loses to themselves.

God put them to tests as they used to undertake the undirected ordinances and remained transgressors. God formed sects and classes among them, some were righteous, and some were tested by good and bad days so that they get corrected. Some of them were given dynasties who took the God sent word but kept following materialistic values.

They remained NA KHALAF and rejected the guidance ultimately to face the wrath of God. The progeny of Adam was given the directives very clearly so that they understand and refrain from the forbidden.

God has many good profiles to remember and follow. Do not keep contact with those who defy the truth. Doomsday will come as a big surprise, about which most of them are not aware.

They labeled the messenger as the knower of the unknown, in which case he would not have been harmed or suffered like any other living being. God procreated a single person, made his mate of like nature to dwell in life with physical and mental peace among themselves.

God created offspring from the process of union to bear a light burden and to grow heavy for happiness and thankfulness, but they again ascribed partners to God and have lost the righteous path.

Follow the way of overlooking other's mistakes, educate them the correct path and avoid terms with illiterates. If obsessed with evil seek God's refuge and when QORAN is read listen with attention, remember God with modesty, humiliation and reverence and do not remain ignorant of the truth.

Fear God, improvise your inter-personal relationships and obey God and the messenger. Believers are those who fear God and listening to QORANIC verses strengthen their faith, put their trust in God, perform regular prayers and spend from the gifts given to them for sustenance.

True believers have grades of dignity, forgiveness and respectful earnings. Recall those times when confronted with enemies, without fighting you won it and got the spoils of war. Recall those times when you requested for unseen help and God approved to send angels, who kept coming for your help rank upon rank.

This was for you to make believe the rulings of God to get contended. Recall those times when you were tranquilized for peace and rain showered upon you for cleansing yourselves and you were imbibed bravery and foundation to plant your feet firmly.

Recall those times when Angels were ordered to support your efforts for succeeding over non believers by devastating their skills.

When you confront the non believers is hostile array, do not turn your backs at them unless you are doing for strategic purpose or returning to seek refuge in preparation of combat, which is permissible. Otherwise punishment is imminent. God help those who hold trust in Him. God can revert the emotions of fear with boldness.

Recall those times when you were oppressed and were living in apprehension of deprivation then God gave you protection, awarded success and provided the best amenities for your sustenance, to remain grateful to God.

Remember that assets and children are tests and trials for you and you will be given the criteria to judge right from wrong and would be awarded with TAQWA, which is a gift from God to seek solace and contentment. In JIHAD continue your efforts with perseverance till the evil is destroyed. Whatever spoils of war you collect keep 1/5th of the share for the sake of God, messenger, relatives, orphans, deserving needy and for the wayfarer.

God reflected in your dream a small number of enemies to keep you unshaken and unimpressed by them and reflected a defensive force suitable for the war and saved you. Remain patient as God approves of patience and perseverance. God does not deny His blessings unless the seekers revert to sin.

Keep prepared for steeds of war but if enemies show inclination for peace then make peace with them. For believers God had been kind in bringing affection and understanding among them.

Oh! Prophet rouse the believers to fight as they are restored with enough courage to vanquish with bigger strengths of enemies. Enjoy what you took in war but which is lawful and good. Those who adopted exile and fought for the cause of God and those who gave the shelter are equal. Help each other in times of need and against the non believers.

Respect the pacts and treaties you have made with others. Form unity among you as non believers are united, otherwise there may be chaos, tumult and riot on earth and great mischief. Importance is for the relations in the family for their rights.

No one tax, defeat or frustrate God. God will convey punishment by shame to them. Except for those disbelievers with whom you have entered into alliance or ties and those who have not harmed you, complete the period of contact with them, as God loves men of words.

But if they ask for forgiveness, perform regular prayers and fine due ZAKATH then they are equal to you. Grant permission for asylum if it is asked as it may keep you nearer to God word. In spite of pacts and contracts if they violate their oaths after covenant and criticize your religion, then counter their attempts and do wage war against them. You will be rewarded in the end.

Do not make friends with disbelievers. They can not establish place in Mosque, as they are misguided in their own faith. God's places of worship are meant for believers, who are righteous and pious and who do not fear anyone except God.

God has showed many victories for believers, including the battle of 'Hunayn', when you were proud of your strengths were tested and had to retreat, but for the true believers who were aided by God's forces and support and succeeded and won the wars.

Spend your energies and money in the path of your religion, unless it is requested with understandable reasons.

There is need for total faith in provisions given by God and to remain contended with it. There is no reward for those who deny the truth and follow religion half heartedly and spend against their wish. God wishes to punish them in this world.

They are cowards and would try escapism. They even try to find fault in charity undertaken by Prophet. They will be happy if they are given some from it and would be angry otherwise. Alms and charity is for the poor and needy, in debtors and those in difficulties and travelers, made compulsory from God.

Those who prefer worldly pleasures and attempts grabbing their part of share from it will be the losers in the end. They started doing misery and undertook delayed tactics, and then God inflicted conflicts in their hearts because they proved evaders and liars.

Those emigrants and ANSAR who are steadfast and righteous and who follow them will honestly are the winners and will be rewarded. There are good and bad people and MUNAFIQEEN will be severely punished. Some are indecisive and seek forgiveness.

You may take alms from them and pray for them. God will see to it.

There are a few who are held in suspicion for whom God had kept the dealings in abeyance. They may be punished or forgiven. Some would side those who would construct Mosque with bad intentions by way of mischief to spread indifference among the pious and give refuge to those who were against the God and his messenger, but God is witness that they are liars.

The mosque is built on foundations of piety and truth and purity as God likes purity.

God appointed the sun a splendor and the moon a light, and measured the stages. God knows the number of the years, and the day of reckoning. Those who believe and do good works, which their Lord guided them by their faith, rivers will flow beneath them in the Gardens of delight.

And if misfortune touches a man he cries towards God, when God relieves him of the misfortune he goes his way as though he had not cried. Then God appointed you viceroys in the earth so that God might see how you behave.

Yet when God had delivered them, they rebel in the earth wrongfully. Your rebellion is only against yourselves. You have enjoyment of the life of the world; then to God is your return and God shall proclaim to you what you used to do .

And God summon to the abode of peace, and lead whom He will to a straight path. Those who do good deeds, get the best reward and more thereafter. Neither dust nor humiliation comes near them. Such are rightful owners of the Garden of delight; where they will abide thereafter.

God provides for you from the sky and the earth, He owns your hearing and sight, and He brings forth the living from the dead and brings forth the dead from the living;

QORAN is not such as could ever be invented; but it is a confirmation of that which was before it and an exposition of that which is decreed for mankind. Times of rewards and punishments are marked and scheduled, otherwise beneficiaries would have got their rewards and the losers would have received their penalties.

Those of them who play tricks and gimmicks with the God's message should know that angels are recording all of your good and bad deeds.

God allows your movement on land and water while riding on boats, carrying you with the help of breezes and you feel privileged, but when these breezes turn into strong winds and they get trapped in high waves, then they call upon God for rescue, and when rescued they turn back to thanklessness, but their attitudes will cause their own suffering in the end.

Worldly life has a few advantages but you will have to return to God ultimately. Whomever God wishes are blessed with His guidance. Those supporting structures which you rely upon and intercessors with God will stand against you and defy your efforts. Most of them are following only the apparent assumptions, but truth has its own convictions and God is aware of everything.

No one is answerable for other's acts, each are responsible for their own deeds. The truth is God does not do injustice, people are their own worst enemies. You have no authority to impose benefit or loss on yourself and neither on others. You are destined to your fate as per God's wish.

Justice will be delivered to those committing cruelty. Every moment God keeps a vigilant watch on you, nothing big or small is is unknown to Him. You have nights for rest and days for observance to know the signs for those who can understand.

If you are inflicted with pain God alone can relieve you of it. God blesses provisions which no one can take away from you. God is kind for all, immaterial of anyone's deeds.

Seek forgiveness from God for all your sins. Do not form intercessors to God. All those who would do good deeds will be rewarded accordingly. God knows your deepest secrets.

God is responsible for feeding all creatures and allocating spaces for them. God allows enjoyment of normalcy to His people, and when He brings downfall from normalcy people get dejected and frustrated.

Whatever happens will be for your own good. Believers should thank God for His blessings and develop tolerance for the deprivations.

Those who wish for worldly glitters are granted comforts in the world, but they will be tested thereafter and shall pay its price without diminution. Those who misguide and find fault with the truth in spite of the senses of hearing and sight will be the losers on the day of judgment.

Many people in Prophet Noah's time did not pay heed to the word of God he conveyed. God ordered him to make an ark and to select species of all creatures, two in kind, male and female, to embark on it, except his wife and his son who did not accept God's verdict and were drowned. Noah and his followers sailed safely.

Those who have forbearance will be sanctioned glad tidings in this world and in the hereafter.

Prophet Hud was sent to guide the people of Aad. Those that followed him were safe and blessed.

For the people of Thamud, Prophet Saleh was sent. Those who believed in his word were saved, and those who did not, perished.

Angels were sent to Prophet Abraham with God's word, and he began to plead for the people of Aad.

Prophet Shoeb was sent to people of Mayan who were cheating with weights and measures, on whom descended the penalty of Ignominy. Moses was sent with the word of God, to which some paid heed and some did not. Their fates were also destined.

Oh! Prophet, Establish firm footing and do not cross limitations, do not incline towards oppressors and do not develop soft corners for the cruel. Pray in segregations with regularity as they compensate for the evil deeds. Be patient as God does not deprive reward of patience.

QORAN is a transcript in Arabic for you to interpret and understand properly. Oh! Prophet, It is sent to you through revelations and is a document of glad tidings as you were unaware of it before.

It is God who raised the heavens without pillars which is evident and with systematized space. He has subordinated the sun and moon and each revolves and rotates in fixed orbits following fixed timings. This is the effect of God, and in it are signs for you to openly interact with God.

He has spread the earth in vastness and erected mountains and flown rivers. He has duplicated gardens of fruits. He hides night over day. Without contradiction, these are the signs for the thinkers and wise people.

Landscapes merge with each other. Some are fertile with gardens of grapes, fields and date palms with branches. Some are barren. All are served water. God created varieties of fruits with distinction, in it are signs for the intelligent.

God has both facets of forgiveness and punishment. Each generation is guided by advisors.

God is knower of the origin in the womb of female and the variation in sizes of the abdomen are by His directions, as he is aware of the obvious and the hidden. He knows what is in still nights and in daylight. God's vigilantes are all around mankind and keep a close watch.

It is God who warns you with thunderbolts and provide you with the hope from heavily laden clouds. He alone let the thunderbolts fall on whomsoever for devastation. All creatures and their shadows pray to God willing or unwilling. God is the one and the ultimate creator and controller.

He showers rains and channels flow, each in their own measure. The foam of the waves equals to the scum of the impurities of the ornaments, which are extinguished in no time.

What remains is for the benefit of the mankind and these are exemplary extensions set out as parables. Those are the righteous that stick to the covenants of God and fail not in their commitments.

They keep relationships intact and fear the terrible reckoning, apprehend the final accountability and remain patient for God's willingness from prayers.

Those who rebel, riot and break the law will be sent to the Hell. God enlarges or limits the provisions for sustenance of livelihood in the World per his wishes, but it's the life hereafter that's important.

QORAN is sent to enlighten you from the darkness. On every race and creed messengers were sent to converse in their own language in order to make things clear to them. God will show the righteous path to whomsoever He wishes. God set examples for the sake of advice.

You cannot count the obligations you have unto God. Do not forget the prayers of Abraham, who sought guidance, forgiveness for his clan, thanked God for the blessings of children Ishmael and Isaac. He prayed and sought pardon for his parents.

God will requite each soul according to its deserts, and God is swift in calling for the account.

God is the inventor of QORAN and will remain its protector and assuredly will guard it.

Those who invade privacy of others and listen behind are devilish and will be subjected to open fire. God cultivated plantations in fixed amounts as provisions of all kinds in due balance. You have no control or capacity to do it on your own for your dependents.

The ecological assets are kept as sources of treasure to be delivered in appropriate ways and ascertainable measures. God allows rains for drinking water and you are not the guardians of its stores.

Humans are created out of mud molded into shape and angels are made out of fire of scorching wind. The evil people will be sent to hell as promised abode to them. Pious believers will be sent to Heaven. They will not be put to any pain forever and will be joyfully put to thrones of dignity.

We bestowed the seven oft repeated verses and the great QORAN, so do not get carried away by distractions and keep soft corners for the believers, who prostrate themselves in adoration.

Turn away from disbelievers who ridicule prophets and form intercessors to the God, and God is aware of your feelings regarding such things.

God had created cattle for your food, comfort, warmth, dress, and numerous other benefits. They are for your decoration, conveyance and transport, riding with heavy loads and created other things which you are knowledgeable about. God showed you the right and wrong path and you may choose from therein.

God also created many living creatures in land and water in different shapes and colors for you to enjoy benefits from. God also created fresh nutrition from water and also ornaments of jewels and pearls, and ships to sail.

It is for you to earn blessings so that you remain grateful. Mountains are erected for your stability and streams to move you to destinations. Beyond doubt you cannot account for the presents and gifts given by God.

God knows what you conceal and what you reveal. Those who do not have faith in the Day of Judgment are those full of pride and God does not like proud people.

You will be accountable for those whom you have misguided and will be answerable for your misdeeds. Some are guided and some are left unguided. You may know the fate of the defaulters.

Those bearing oppression when migrating from homelands will be given better placements in the world and even better in the hereafter.

In times of suffering you call upon God for help and on getting it and finding relief you revert back to your original behavior. Those who damage and undermine the position of the female offspring are following an evil choice. Those who lie will face a painful doom.

There are cattle for you with instructive signs, they provide milk from which you derive nutrition. From grape fruit wine is produced and it is yet another sign for the intelligent.

God made honeybees to form nests in hills, trees and high roofed habitations, and provide honey which has medicinal value. This is a definite sign for the thinkers.

God promoted some over the other in amenities and richness, and bestowed gifts of sustenance more freely on some of you than the others. They are bound to share their assets among the subordinates and slaves.

God orders for justice, goodness and consideration for the relatives, and restriction from shameful, indecent, or cruel acts. Commitments made in the name of God should not be broken, as God is witness to it. God is all knower, do not take oaths for deception among yourself.

Given words are to be kept honorable otherwise others may repeat the same and non-believers may blame you and deny accepting your faith. Do not break ties, pacts and bonds for trivialities, if you have wisdom. Be patient as patience will have good rewards.

Liars are those who lack faith in the God and prefer worldly life over the life hereafter, and they will be at a big disadvantage in the end.

You are forbidden from eating dead animals, blood, and flesh of swine. Remember that you should not attempt casual remarks about the religious directives and comment upon incompletely understood concepts about God, otherwise you will not become successful.

Those who do bad deeds in ignorance and then genuinely seek forgiveness to correct them will be pardoned. Form a day in a week as auspicious and for Muslims Friday is granted better.

In case of revenge, take at most as much as you are pained for and do not exceed, but it is better still to be tolerant. God is with them who restrain themselves.

God with purity carried the messenger in night from the sacred mosque to the distant mosque and showered blessings around him. He showed some signs of nature, which is known to God alone.

You would do good or bad deeds for your own good or bad. History denoted that those who obeyed God were rewarded and those who did not were punished. Human nature has urgency in its attitude that in times of suffering he curses, but God does not accept it.

On the Day of Judgment all the records of good or bad deeds will be evident of clear knowledge of all. God had devastated many generations for the lesson to the following generations.

Those who believe in the last day do their duties and are respectful of faith in God. God showers amenities for all including believers and non-believers and proved in the world credence over one another, but credence in life hereafter is superior.

Keep obligations for parents if either of them attains old age and dependent on you. Keep caring and respecting them and say not a word of contempt nor repel them. Keep praying for them in humility and submission for the sake of God's kindness as they have cared for you in childhood.

Respect the rights of the relatives, those in want, the underprivileged and wayfarers, but squander not in the manner of spendthrift. Avoid unnecessary extravagance and expense as the extravagant are the friends of evil. If you are awaiting the expected returns from God and are presently incapable to help them, then apologize with pity and tenderness and explain softly and properly to them. Keep balance in your dealings, neither be very miserly nor very lavish.

Be warned that illicit relationships are prohibited, as they are shameful acts and a bad pretense. No one is permitted to take the life of another and the victim's heirs are given the authority to demand QISAS, or forgiveness and are protected by the power of revenge in the same manner without exceeding in limits.

Return the assets of orphans when they attain the age of full strength and are given liabilities and commitments when will be thoroughly assessed. And pursue not the directives about which you have no knowledge and do not boast or show pride nor walk on the earth with insolence as you have limitations. This is not approved by God.

The seven heavens, the earth and the angels are praising God, but you cannot understand this praise. God knows your intentions in any manner you enact. Some would inquire as how after death, when bones and leftovers would disintegrate, could God resurrect and bring them back to life.

While discussing with others use soft and tender words and reasoning and logic. Prophet David was given ZUBUR. God had given privileges to the children of Adam and even graded them higher among other creatures.

Pray to God for the right guidance and to provide power, strength and help. You forget God in times of comfort and call for Him in times of distress. Each one does what is predisposed in his personality and God knows the truth. God has described every example and sign for all in his book.

Prophethood is given to one of your kind and not to any supernatural force, but mankind is narrow minded. God had given nine miracles to Moses. God had sent his messenger with glad tidings and warnings.

QORAN is sent in piecemeal fashion for the Apostle to preach in steps and revealed to him in stages. QORAN teaches humility, subtleness, modesty with clarity of faith and belief. Perform regular prayers neither loudly nor weakly, keep it balanced and seek a middle course.

Nor say "I shall be sure to do so and so tomorrow". Never postpone your liabilities and commitments and vocalize "If God willing", as you are not aware of its happening. Pray for God's guidance.

Those of them stayed in the cave for 309 years but God alone knows the truth. Keep reading QORAN directives which cannot be reversed. Keep company of pious people who worship all the time. Never listen to those who have neglected worship and live solely in worldly pleasures.

Prophet Zakariyah was aged and sought an heir. God cured his wife's barrenness and gave him progeny who was named Yahya. Yahya was given wisdom since childhood and was bestowed consideration, purity, piety, and was made the caretaker of his parents.

Mariam was blessed with a son Jesus, who spoke and admitted that he is given God sent word and prophethood and was the caretaker of his mother. Prophet Abraham left his family, home and intercessors. He was blessed by prophet Isaac and prophet Ishmael with. Prophet Moses' brother Aaron was also given prophethood so also prophet Idris.

Moses prayed to enlighten his wisdom to allow his responsibilities of work to be made easier, to remove the impediments from his speech to carry meaningful understanding for others, to let his minister be from his clan, to let his brother share his tasks and to let both pray to God. God sanctioned all the requests and allowed his upbringing in the palace of Pharaoh and provided the milk from his original mother for living. God had allowed Moses to perform miracles.

God also forgave the unintentional killing of one person and awarded prophesy at an appropriate time. Remember, he he practices lies never succeeds. God wished you to avail what is given to you and to live in modesty without exceeding limits.

Pray to God to let you acquire more knowledge. Forgetting God would lead to hardships in life.

Whenever you find peace of mind, return home. There is weight in truth and truth will always succeed over lies. You are not answerable to anyone except God for your acts or deeds. We put you to test through hardships and comforts.

Human being has urgency in his nature and he is a creature in haste, but you remain patient and tolerant. Beyond doubt the righteous will be protected and will enjoy provisions. Even big stresses and crisis will not cause him any grief or depression.

CHAPTER 9

F ear God. Beyond doubt the day of reckoning is a tremendous thing. Whoever gets acquainted with Satan will be be led astray and will face the wrath of fire.

If you are in doubt about life after death, you may register that you are made out of dust, with mingled fluids, then blood was circulated into you and then flesh was formed with ambiguous appearance and you were kept in the mother's womb for an appointed time. God brought you up in infancy and carried you forward to adulthood.

Some are brought death prematurely and some are carried till old age with dementia, the worst part of life. Believe that God does not do any harm to people otherwise. Those who remain indecisive to pray are craving for the worldly benefits and when put to test revert back and they will be lifting the burden of loss in both the lives.

QORAN is sent with manifest signs. God showers guidance on whom he wishes. On the day of reckoning, for the believers of all philosophies God will give His judgment.

Prophet Abraham was assigned to the house of God (Kaaba) to keep it pure and clean, to organize regular prayers and encircle around it. Announce the pilgrimage of HAJJ for all to visit for their own benefit and sacrifice the denoted class of cattle in the name of God and relish it yourself and give to the needy people and the distressed. Then clean yourself, undertake the promises and perform the circuits.

The articles of HAJJ are God's verdict. Avoid indulging in lies and do not take intercessors to God, avail the profits till a time and complete the rituals. Your piety and righteousness reaches God, glad tidings to you.

For sure believers got the guidance to bring dedication in regular prayers, who turn away from the unnecessary and unimportant things, who pay their taxes and alms, who do not get into infidelity except their wives and owned maids, as they are exempted from the blame. Those who ask for anything more are crossing boundaries.

Those who keep their trusts and covenants and those who are strict in observance of their regular prayers are the inheritors of heaven where they will remain forever.

For sure God had made human beings from the elements of Earth, then formed mingled fluids from such elements and preserved it for safety, then made it into a clot of compact cells, cells into tissues, tissues into organs, then formed bones and clothed the bones with flesh.

Then you all will be subjected to death and will be resurrected on the doom's day. God made seven heavens above you and God is not ignorant about the creations. In correct proportions and method He shower rains from sky and let it stay in the Earth and God has control over its density.

From the same source God provide you with date palm fruits and grape gardens and many other fruits which you relish. He created a tree from the rock of Mount Sinai which produces oil, which you use as sauce in food.

The existence of cattle and animals is also a big lesson for you, milk is produced from them for you and many other useful amenities and you are allowed to eat meat from a few of them. Cattle and boats are made means of transport.

God sent messengers. Leaders of the tribes who were given privileged positions denied the truth of the Apostle and the day of reckoning, in spite of the leader being a man himself, who eats and drinks like any other person. Those who do not obey God will be put to loss by Him.

God created many other races and prophets for guidance with dignity and grace. He always gives allowance of some time for all to get corrected. Righteous are those who spend from their wealth and feel fear of committing any negligence in giving them to the needy. God does not give suffering and pain to the one who cannot bear it.

Do you think God had created human beings for no reason and that you will not be returned back?

Those who are wise and broadminded should continue to give permissiveness among kindred and forgive relatives, needy and immigrants as you want God to forgive you for your mistakes.

Mischievous and KHABEES males and females are best suited for themselves and pure men and women are best suited for themselves. Keep a note that before entering other's homes do not do unless permitted and unless you salute them to signify your announcement of entry.

If you do not get any reply from the inmates, do not enter and if asked to return back, do so as this is the best way of doing. If a house is not occupied and you have some provision or need in it then you can enter in it. Your intention is known to God.

God asks men and women to keep their gazes low.

Women are prescribed a scarf over their heads and be mindful of exposing their glamor, except for in presence of their husbands, fathers or father-in-laws, sons or husband's sons or brothers or nephews or female acquaintances or servants who are devoid of sexual appetite, or children.

Among you those of men and women who are not married arrange their NIKAHS among widows among you, as God will grant means from His bounty and measures or their sustenance.

Mosques are esteemed and exalted by the grace of God, undertake prayers to glorify God. Those involved in business transactions, which do not interfere with their piety and worship, will be rewarded with returns in excess.

God had created creatures out of His resources, which crawl and walk on two limbs and walk on four limbs. God can undertake what he wishes. There are hypocrites who keep changing their roles, attitudes and behaviors for self-gratifications and deny the truth thereafter.

Believers and good doers will be made viceroys on Earth and with true faith they will be made rulers and they will exchange peace and security with fear.

Those of you who are handicapped can take the freedom of seeking their food from all their relatives and friends, but pass on salutation before entry in the homes. Do not call Prophet as you call upon others among you, as they are given dignity and position.

God had given his messenger an ordinary status and had sent earlier messengers with similar limitations, but all these are tests for you. Those who feel great about themselves are transgressors and would be like dust particles, but on the day of reckoning heaven dwellers will be better posted in their resting places. On that day angels will be sent in continuous succession and God alone will have control.

God had sent His word in stages and recited it in steps so that its retention gets completed. The people astray have formed their idols for their own satisfaction. They will never find the right guidance, as they are like animals or even worse than them.

God had made your shadows as signs, which contracts with the rising sun and get evaded by nights. He has made night for rest and sleep and day for work, He sends cool breezes as indications for rains which are showered in sprays at different places in different times which in itself is a sign and which brings life from the dead soil.

God had created two kinds of water which are united, one is sweet and palatable and the other is salty, and there is a partition between them. God had kept your own relatives and in-laws for whom you are committed. Seek advice from knowledgeable and wise.

Keep distance from those who are ignorant and engage in discussions. Those who spend their wealth neither extravagantly nor miserly and spend in a balanced way are the righteous. Neither do they form intercessor with God nor do they kill, or indulge in adultery, as all these acts will have their own disgrace.

Those who do not give false witness keep away from unwanted situations and when QORANIC verses are chanted they simply do not believe blindly. They seek and pray that their wives and children should bring solace and contentment for them, they will be granted heaven.

The heir of Prophet David was Solomon, who could converse with and understand the chanting of birds.

Patience and tolerance double returns. This will replace evil with goodness. When irrelevant talks are held some remain aloof, they say our deeds are for ourselves and your deeds are for you and peace be upon you, we do not indulge in arguments with ignorant. These are people with good deeds, and will reap good returns.

Prophet Lut was the brother of Prophet Abraham and Prophet Mohamed was the progeny of Prophet Ishmael. Do not argue with AHL AL KITAB, unless with logic and reasoning. Those who struggle take efforts in the correct path will be guided in the proper direction.

Following the religious way you may be subjected to difficulties, tasks and problems. Continue doing EHSAAN. Do good deeds with sincerity, and respect other's rights. God does not go back on His promises, they will be fulfilled in time.

They are only acquainted with the apparent charms of the worldly pleasures but are not aware of the life thereafter. A man's enemy is his own self and God does not do any harm. Your mates are created among you for love and affection and for your tranquility and happiness.

There are signs in different races with different colors and creeds. Nights are for rest and relaxation and day for seeking God's blessings in the form of provisions. People enjoy the gift of God and on their own faults they become hopeless.

The interest on money lending which increases in quantum does not increase in the measure of God. The tax and charity which you give will be returned to you manifold. If one oppresses another human being riots are resulted, but they reap the fruits of what they do, so that they correct themselves. God is compelled to help the believers. God brings you up in weakness; gives strength and then weakness again. Keep faith and patience.

Some people get into wasteful recreations. They misguide out of ignorance and ridicule, but they are going to be punished with defamation. Even plants are cultivated by genders.

Luqman advised his son that God directed the people to respect and care for the parents, that mother is given an important position for her efforts of child bearing and rearing and milking the infant for two years. Remain thankful to parents and also obedient. If they deviate from God do not get influenced by their disbelief, but keep caring for them.

Perform prayers and keep patience in hardships. Do not expose pride, do not be boastful, keep balance in your pace of walking, keep your voice and tone low and do not shout. People quarrel among themselves because of insufficient understanding of God's directives.

Those who have faith in God's revelations, who prostrate before God, praise the almighty, do not show pride, they call upon God with fear and hope and spend whatever is gifted by God. God will test people by small and petty worldly sickness and problems for their correction.

If mistakes are committed out of innocence then there is no sin. Willful intention of sin is different. Messenger is given dignity and position over others. Wives of messenger are the mothers of Muslims. Relatives also have an upper degree of relationship than acquaintances. Keep good conduct and etiquette with friends.

Believers are put to test in wars and in suffering. Do not use your verbal communication to undermine others. Do not remain greedy. In times of distress remain steadfast as you never know how God's strategy will help and support you.

God's gifts are innumerable and incomparable. Those believing men and women who are obedient, patient, modest, charitable, chaste, faithful and shameful will be rewarded by God. Apostle is declared the last prophet on the Earth. Do not worry about hardships faced by you from the non-believers. Keep faith in God and God will find a way to cause relief.

If you marry a Muslim woman and have not mated with her, then you are not bonded by the SHARIA LAW to pay MAHR (Mandatory Payment) or any other alimony and women are not bonded by the period of three menstrual cycles of IDDAT (Waiting period after husbands demise or divorce). Better still is to part whatever you can afford or half of the MAHR.

Apostle kept justice in divisibility of time with his wives and he in illness sought permission with wives to remain with Ayesha.

The people of Saba were given gifts for thankfulness, which they denied and faced God's wrath. Those who remain indecisive and unsure about the directives are the ones who will be caught in disgrace and harm. You are directed to think by yourself or to seek advice from others.

CHAPTER 10

P rophet may warn the people who are ignorant, but some of them will still not believe, even if they are warned or not. God will resurrect the dead and will record the acts and deeds they did for others.

Everything is documented in the book. God has created pairs in the creatures, including plantations, even which you are not aware of. God grants blessings for a predetermined time span.

On the last day nothing will be done extraneously, or out of revenge or aggression, except accountability of the done acts and deeds.

You will be rewarded for your good deeds in Heaven, you will be given wine from an overflowing stream, which you will relish, without getting intoxicated and you will be provided partners with enchanting beauty.

God had not created universe without a purpose. Those of them whose forefathers had been astray, tried following them as their role models. Prophet Noah was from the chosen few and God had given salutations to him. Prophet Abraham was his follower, who warned the disbelievers that how come they worship the idols which they have handcrafted.

The people in anger and frustration wanted to throw him in the fire, but God rescued him. Abraham was given orders to sacrifice his son, who expressed his willingness to be sacrificed and at the time of execution God replaced a sacrificial animal.

Prophet Younus was swallowed by a fish upon an err committed by him and he would have remained inside till the dooms day, if he has not asked for forgiveness and had not worshipped God in continuity so he was kept alive and governed the message of God.

Swearing upon this book of guidance, races before these were perished and cried in agony, but it was late and destined time was in-escapable. They doubted the revelations.

Remember Prophet David who was powerful and submitted totally to God and we subordinated mountains to pray along with him and birds were also subordinated. We gave stability and strength to his rule and gave him the capability of tact and wisdom. God had not created the universe without reason.

Prophet Solomon was the son of Prophet David. They being human beings were committed to err but sought forgiveness and were pardoned. Prophet Solomon was blessed by control over breezes and some supernatural things were also gifted to him.

Prophet Ayub was among the tolerant and patient.

God is indifferent about your thanklessness, He likes thankfulness. It is improbable that the intelligent and the unintelligent could be equal. Only the intelligent gets the guidance.

Those who do good deeds will get good returns and patient people will get even better returns. God had bestowed on you this best book which is not dissimilar with other books and has repetitive verses which warn people who fear god. Thereafter they become docile and soft hearted by God's grace.

We have described several of many examples to them to get the required guidance. They accept what is destined and that is TAWAKKUL (Reliance).

When mankind gets into hardships they call upon God's favors and when they are rewarded they boast about the relief having been brought by their wisdom, but even rewards including wisdom is a test by God. So you are warned to perform good deeds before you are put to trial. Those of you who are proud will be sent to hell.

The angels worship and pray God. They also pray for the forgiveness, guidance and success of believers. You are ordained to ask from God and you are promised that God will listen and grant you what is asked for.

God had sent messengers about some of them you are informed and for some you are not. Prophets can not execute miracles with out the will of God.

God had created creatures on Earth in two days and amenities and provisions for the needy inhabitants were created in four days with equity, then turned towards the skies, which was a smoke and made seven skies in two days and decorated it with lamps and protection.

Whomever God wishes will provide the provisions in excess. Those who prefer the reaps of the life hereafter will be given accordingly and those who prefer the reaps of the life in this world will be given accordingly, but not the gifts thereafter.

Keep considerations for the relationships. The hardships and sufferings one faces is all due to one's own misdeeds, God otherwise had always been kind.

Those who confide in God and refrain from shameful and sinful things, those who forgive others even during episodes of anger and vengeance, accept God's verdict in any case, perform regular prayers, act after due consultations and agreements among themselves and give charity and alms out of the gifted wealth and when oppressed feel courage to avenge up to an extent but prefer to forgive are the true believers.

It is upon God's directives that cattle are put under your subordination, otherwise you would not have had the power to tame them.

Beyond doubt Prophet Jesus is the sign of the doom's day. On the day of reckoning the thickest friends among the astray will become enemies, but the pious and the obedient will be free from fear and depression. You and your wives will be happily living in the heaven.

God is fully aware of all acts done by mankind, but they are not aware of it. They are also ignorant of the fact that every action of there is being recorded. Those deserving of the blessings are the ones who stick to truth and are the wise.

QORAN is sent to you on an auspicious night. On that night further decisions will be taken. BANI ISRAEL were the privileged among the people of their times and we had put them to tests and trials.

God had not created life between sky and Earth just for the game sake. There had been a purpose and strategy behind it, but most of them were ignorant.

The changing directions of the winds are signs for the wise and intelligent. Pretentious, exhibitionistic and those with pride are the receivers of the painful doom.

Believers should avoid disbelievers. QORAN is a complete ordinance of life to be lived on and guidance sought for glad tidings. Those who are enslaved by their wishful thinking are the misguided and those who consider right are actually wrongly guessing their distinctions.

The age of adulthood is 40 years.

Those who claim to have been fed up of their parents will be punished severely. You will be designated according to your deeds. Those who profit from worldly pleasures will be losers. Rebellious and proud can not make the God helpless.

On having believed on God sent word and His messenger, the believers will be forgiven for their past sins committed in the past. God wants to test each other from one another.

As of those who disbelieve and turn away from God, He shall render their works ineffective. And as for those who believe and do good and believe in what is revealed to MOHAMED and it is the truth from their Lord, He will remove evil from them and improve their condition.

The worldly life is just a game, but if you have faith and TAQWA then you will be rewarded. You are among those who spend your earnings in the path of God and are not miser. A few of them do become misers, but they are doing harm to themselves.

God is the giver and you are the receiver and if you disbelieve then you will be replaced by believers.

God had blessed you with success. He had created patience and tolerance in the believers and increases their faith. Those who break heir promises they are actually breaking promises for themselves.

Hypocrites find excuses and say what they do not mean. It would remain God's will to react to their acts. Do not agree with them and do not support them. You will be awarded success over things which you have not acquired before. God's strategy is different. He had brought calm and tranquility for Muslims and you succeeded in the end and messenger's word is proved righteous.

Do not surpass or exceed the messenger. Fear God. Do not raise the pitch of your voice above the voice of the messenger. Do not talk with him in rough tone. Those who call upon him loudly are unintelligent people.

If an evil doer extends some information, then first find out the truth after research, so that you do not harm anyone in ignorance and would then repent for it.

If two Muslim groups get into conflict, then help to reach a compromise. If one group is oppressing the other, you take the side of the oppressed and resist the oppression. Do justice and compromise with balance.

All Muslims are brethren among one another and they should be brought close to each other. Do not ridicule others as you do not know if they are better than you. Do not find fault with others, neither swear bad names to others.

Oh! Believers safeguard you with doubts and suspicions, as they are same as sins. Neither be after other's weakness for exploitation, as it not recommended. Only one who fears God is the most respectful. Correct yourself in the hope of seeking forgiveness. You cannot show off piety to God, as God is all knower.

We created mankind and we know what they think and God is close with them. One who prevents you from doing good deeds, who exceeds limits, who is suspicious and who talks without certification, will be questioned. Those who are negligent and unaware would ask about the Day of Judgment.

The righteous used to sleep less, worship in the mornings and used to keep the shares of those who avoid asking openly. Keep guiding and advising others.

Those who have faith and whose children have faith will be sent to Heaven. Each one will get what he deserves.

Do not praise yourself as God knows the best.

We have made QORAN easy to understand. You have to get the guidance out of it.

Mankind had been given superiority over other creatures. Planets are orbit rated and worship God. God exalted measurements in balance to disallow exceeding. God had spread the Earth for the inhabitants to cherish fruits, cereals and fragrant flowers. Created two rivers to merge with a partition, out of which pearls and shells will be brought out, ships are allowed to sail on seas. Those of you with faith will be respected. We will soon attend towards you. Sinners will be identified by their faces.

Heavens have branches, two heavens with two springs, in which two types fruits will be available. Two more heavens other than these with greeneries of date palms and pomegranates will be there. God is great. Which among these blessings and gifts from God could be denied?

Spend from the bestowed wealth, as you are the trustee for the deserving. Charity will be rewarded. Remember that the worldly life is only a game. People express pride and boast high about their children and their assets, should know that it is temporary. You avoid becoming sorrowful upon grief after death of kith and kin. Neither exhibit elation on the gifted things, as it is disliked by God.

Those who do misery and advice the same to others are turned away from faith. God is indifferent about such things. For sure messengers were sent with open and glad tidings, with books and true balances, so that people stick to justice.

Whispers are not good etiquette. Whisper only the good words. God had given you wealth without bloodshed for the sake of God, prophet, relatives, orphans, needy and wayfarers so that, wealth does not get accumulated. The spoils of the war are for the emigrants and needy, who left their homes and properties for the sake of God and sought God's willingness and helped the Prophet and in turn God. Such are the righteous people.

Those who developed faith, had a liking for the emigrants, preferred them over themselves, did not feel constriction for them, and whoever seeks relief from their own self gratifications are the winners.

Oh! Believers you frighten them as they are ignorant. They appear united but they actually have differences among themselves.

Those of you, who had not fought with you for the religion, keep relationship with them and do justice, as God loves those who do justice.

Oh! Believers what ever you commit, why you did not complete it and what you can not do should not be committed.

Prophet Jesus, son of Mary announced the good news of the next apostle to come, whose name is Ahmed, but people did not believe him. God sent the last Prophet to make believe.

Oh! Believers when you are called for JUMA (Friday) Prayers leave your trading and go to pray.

Your children and your assets are your tests.

Life and death is your trial.

Do not value those who are in habit of swearing oaths. They are SARKASH (Headstrong) because of wealth and children.

Pray in the night and read QORAN. For sure you remain busy in the day. Leave the liars and stricken people and give them time.

God is aware of the fact that praying in night could not be succumbed, so read and pray as much as you can. Your good deeds will be blessed by better rewards.

God give guidance to whomever he wishes.

QORAN is for guidance, whoever wants can seek it. Guidance can be sought when God decrees it.

It is wrong to cheat in weights and measures in trade. Wrong doers when they intend to take, they take it to the maximum and when they intend to give they attempt restrictions. Those who deny the word of God are the sinners.

God had been merciful on you. So do not be harsh on the orphans nor on the needy who are asking for your help.

Surely hardships are always followed by comforts. When you get leisure, work for your religion.

Badly destined are those who find fault with others and does back biting. Those who count and gather wealth are under the misunderstood conception that wealth will be forever.

PART IV

AHADITH GUIDELINES

CHAPTER 11

"**I**f ALLAH wants to do good to a person, He makes him comprehend the religion. I am just a distributor, but the grant is from ALLAH.

"Facilitate good things to people and do not make it hard for them to follow and give them good tidings and do not make them run away."

"Be like, a person, whom ALLAH has given wealth and he spends it righteously; the one whom ALLAH has given wisdom and he acts according to it and teaches it to others."

"Some of you make others dislike good deeds. So whoever leads the people in prayer should shorten it because among them there are the sick the weak and the needy of time."

"Do not tell a lie intentionally then he will surely enter the Hell-fire."

"Faith consists of branches. 'HAYA' is one of them which encompasses self respect, modesty, bashfulness, and scruple, as a part of faith."

"A Muslim is the one, who avoids harming Muslims with his tongue and hands.i.e. With speech and actions."

"Good deeds of Islam are: To feed and greet those whom you know and those whom you do not know, if you can afford."

"None of you will have faith till he wishes for his Muslim brother what he likes for himself."

"Do not join anything in worship along with ALLAH. Do not steal. Do not commit adultery. Do not accuse an innocent person and spread it among people. Do not be disobedient towards good deeds."

"Whoever has the following four characters will be a hypocrite, until he gives it up. These are: (1) Whenever he talks, he tells a lie; (2) whenever he makes a promise, he breaks it; (3) whenever he makes a covenant he proves treacherous; (4) and whenever he quarrels, he behaves impudently in an evil insulting manner."

"Whoever observes fasts during the month of Ramadan out of sincere faith, and hoping to attain rewards, then all his past sins will be forgiven."

"Religion is very easy and whoever overburdens himself in it will not be able to continue in that way. So you should not be extremists, but try to be near to perfection and receive the good tidings that you will be rewarded."

"If any one of you improves his Islamic principles, then his good deeds will be rewarded many times, for each good deed and a bad deed will be recorded as it is."

"Do good deed which are within your capacity and the best acts of Worship in the sight of ALLAH are that which are done regularly."

"A believer who accompanies the funeral procession of a Muslim out of sincere faith and hoping to attain ALLAH's reward and remains with it till the funeral prayer is offered and the burial ceremonies are over, he will return with a reward."

"Both legal and illegal things are evident but in between them there are doubtful things and most of the people have no knowledge about them. So whoever saves himself from these suspicious things saves his religion and his honor. And whoever indulges in these suspicious things is going astray."

"If a man spends on his family sincerely for ALLAH's sake then it is a kind of alms-giving in reward for him".

"If a woman gives in charity from her house meals without wasting and being extravagant, she will get the reward for her giving, and her husband will also get the reward for his earning and the keeper will also get a similar reward. The acquisition of the reward of none of them will reduce the reward of the others."

"Whoever desires an expansion in his sustenance and age, should keep good relations with his Kith and kin."

"Nobody has ever eaten a better meal than that which one has earned by working with one's own hands".

"Do not urge somebody to return what he has already bought in optional sale from another seller so as to sell him your own goods."

"The honest treasurer who gives willingly what he is ordered to give, is one of the two charitable persons, the second being the owner."

"Procrastination and delay in repaying debts by a wealthy person is injustice."

"Whoever takes the money of the people with the intention of repaying it, ALLAH will repay it on his behalf, and whoever takes it in order to spoil it, then ALLAH will spoil him."

"If someone leaves some property, it will be for the inheritors, and if he leaves some weak offspring, it will be for us to support them."

"ALLAH has forbidden for you, (1) to be undutiful to your mothers, (2) to undermine your daughters, (3) to not to pay the rights of the others and (4) to beg of men for living."

"Every one of you is a guardian, and responsible for what is in his custody. The ruler is a guardian of his subjects and responsible for them; a husband is a guardian of his family and is responsible for it; a lady is a guardian of her husband's house and is responsible for it, and a servant is a guardian of his master's property and is responsible for it." and "A man is a guardian of his father's property and is responsible for it, so all of you are guardians and responsible for your wards and things under your care."

"A Muslim is a brother of another Muslim, so he should not oppress him, nor should he hand him over to an oppressor. Whoever fulfilled the needs of his brother, ALLAH will fulfill his needs; whoever brought his Muslim brother out of a discomfort, ALLAH will bring him out of the discomforts of the Day of Resurrection."

"Good religious practices are (1) To pay a visit to the sick or inquire about his health, (2) to follow funeral processions, (3) to say to a sneezer, "May ALLAH be merciful to you", (4) to return greetings, (5) to help the oppressed, (6) to accept invitations, (7) to help others to fulfill their oaths."

"The most hated person in the sight of ALLAH is the most quarrelsome person."

"No-one should prevent his neighbor from fixing a wooden peg in his wall."

"The reward of deeds depends upon the intentions and every person will get the reward according to what he has intended. So whoever emigrated for worldly benefits or for a woman to marry, his emigration was for what he emigrated for."

"For mourning, he who slaps his cheeks, tears his clothes and follows the ways and traditions of the Days of Ignorance is not one of us."

"You'd better leave your inheritors wealthy rather than leaving them poor, begging others. You will get a reward for whatever you spend for ALLAH's sake."

"If any one of you see a funeral procession and he is not going along with it, then he should stand and remain standing till he gets behind it, or it leaves him behind, or the coffin is put down before it goes ahead of him."

"Those are the worst creatures in the Sight of ALLAH, who whenever a pious man dies amongst them, make a place of worship at his grave."

"I shall accept the invitation even if I was invited to a meal of a sheep's trotter, and I shall accept the gift even if it were a trotter of a sheep."

"Accept gifts and give something in return."

"Give in charity and do not give reluctantly lest ALLAH should give you in a limited amount; and do not withhold your money lest ALLAH should withhold it from you."

"The best amongst you is he who pays back his debt in the most handsome way.'

"Save yourself from Hell-fire even by giving half a date-fruit in charity."

"The charity which you wish to practice does not delay it to the time of approaching death."

"Seven people will be shaded by ALLAH (1) a just ruler; (2) a young man who has been brought up in the worship of ALLAH; (3) a man whose heart is attached to the mosque; (4) two persons who love each other only for ALLAH's sake and they meet and part in ALLAH's cause only; (6) a person who practices charity so secretly that his left hand does not know what his right hand has given and (7) a person who remembers ALLAH in seclusion and his eyes get flooded with tears."

"The best charity is that which is practiced by a wealthy person, and start giving first to your dependents."

"From the money which is left after his expenses, give charity to whoever abstains from asking others for some financial help, ALLAH will give him and save him from asking others".

"It is better for anyone of you to take a rope and cut and bring a bundle of wood from the forest over his back and sell it and ALLAH will save his face because of that, rather than to ask the people who may give him or not."

"ALLAH has hated for you three things: 1. Vain and useless talk that you talk too much or about others. 2. Wasting of wealth by extravagance 3. And asking too many questions in disputed religious matters or asking others for something even if not in great need".

"The great sins are 1) To join others in worship with ALLAH, (2) To be undutiful to one's parents. (3) To commit the crime of murdering. (4) And to give a false witness."

"He, who makes peace between the people by inventing good information or saying good things, is not a liar."

"No Muslim should offer more for a thing already bought by his Muslim brother, nor should he demand the hand of a girl already engaged to another Muslim. A Muslim woman shall not try to bring about the divorce of another Muslim woman in order to take her place herself."

"Those who do good deeds will get the reward for it and also the reward of others who follow him and continue doing good deeds."

"After death 3 things remain 1.knowledge and literacy which could enlighten the next generation, 2.Righteous children to pray for the deceased parents 3. Charitable trusts which would benefit the next generations."

"The young should greet the old, the passerby should greet the sitting one, and the small group of persons should greet the large group of persons."

"A man should not make another man get up from the latter's seat in a gathering in order to sit there."

"When three persons are together, then no two of them should hold secret counsel excluding the third person."

"Riches do not mean, having a great amount of property, but riches are self-contentment with what one is blessed with."

"A believer is relieved by death from the troubles and hardships of the world and lives for the Mercy of ALLAH, while the death of a wicked person relieves the other people, the surroundings and the animals."

"If any ruler having the authority to rule Muslim subjects dies while he is deceiving them, ALLAH will forbid Paradise for him."

"None of you should long for death, for if he is a good man, he may increase his good deeds, and if he is an evil-doer, he may stop the evil deeds and repent thereafter".

"ALLAH wrote in His Book – 'My Mercy overpowers My Anger'."

"Any person who takes a piece of land unjustly will sink down the seven earths on the Day of Resurrection."

"The sun and the moon are two signs amongst the Signs of ALLAH. They do not eclipse because of some reason. So, if you see them in eclipse, celebrate the Praises of ALLAH and pray."

"If somebody keeps a dog that is neither used for farm work nor for guarding the livestock, he will lose one the reward of his good deeds every day."

"ALLAH will not look on the Day of Judgment at him who drags his robe behind him out of pride."

"The prescribed Law of ALLAH is the equality in punishment". "Alcoholic drinks are extracted from five things: Grapes, dates, honey, wheat and barley. And they confuse and stupefy the mind."

"Ask not about things which, if made plain to you, may cause you trouble."

"The best women are the riders of the camels and the righteous among the women are the kindest women to their children in their childhood and the more careful women of the property of their husbands."

"A woman is married for four things, i.e., her wealth, her family status, her beauty and her religion. So you should marry the religious woman and prioritize these qualities in reverse order."

"And none should ask for the hand of a girl who is already engaged to his Muslim brother, but one should wait till the first suitor marries her or leaves her."

"Set the captives free, accept the wedding invitation and visit the patients."

"Women have been allowed to go out for their needs."

"If the wife of anyone of you asks permission to go to the mosque, he should not forbid her."

"Dislike that one, who goes to one's family at night on returning from a journey."

"It is not lawful for a Muslim woman who believes in ALLAH and the Last Day to mourn for more than three days, except for her husband, for whom she should mourn for four months and ten days."

"The best alms is that which you give when you are rich, and you should start first to support your dependants."

"Alcoholic drinks are prohibited and all drinks that intoxicate are unlawful to drink."

CHAPTER 12

"When you drink water, do not breathe in the vessel; and when you urinate or defecate, do not use your right hand."

"No fatigue, nor disease, nor sorrow, nor sadness, nor hurt, nor distress befalls a Muslim, even if it were the prick he receives from a thorn, but that ALLAH expiates some of his sins for that."

"If ALLAH wants to do good to somebody, He afflicts him with trials."

"You are warned against giving forged statement and a false witness."

"Your slaves are your brothers and ALLAH has put them under your command. So whoever has a brother under his command should feed him of what he eats and dress him of what he wears. Do not ask them to do things beyond their capacity and if you do so, then help them".

"Do not revert to disbelief after me by striking the necks of one another."

"Whoever abstains from asking others, ALLAH will make him contented, and whoever tries to make he self-sufficient, ALLAH will make him self-sufficient. And whoever remains patient, ALLAH will make him patient. Nobody can be given a blessing better and greater than patience."

A beggar is not the only poor person. There are people who are silent about their conditions but do not have enough money for their needs. These people deserve charity.

"A time will come when one will not care how one gains one's money, legally or illegally."

"Allah's mercy will be on him who is lenient in his buying, selling, and in demanding back his money."

"The buyer and the seller have the option to cancel or to confirm the deal, as long as they have not parted or till they part, and if they spoke the truth and told each other the defects of the things, then blessings would be in their deal, and if they hid something and told lies, the blessing of the deal would be lost".

"I will be an opponent to three types of people on the Day of Resurrection: 1. One who makes a covenant in My Name, but proves treacherous; 2. One who sells a free person and eats his price; and 3. One who employs a laborer and takes full work from him but does not pay him for his labour."

"The best amongst you is the one who pays the rights of others generously."

"ALLAH has forbidden for you, (1) to be undutiful to your mothers, (2) to bury your daughters alive, (3) to not to pay the rights of the others and (4) to beg of men."

"Good tidings are the lowering of your gazes on seeing what is illegal to look at, refraining from harming people, returning greetings, advocating good and forbidding evil."

"The foster relations are treated like blood relations in marital affairs."

"There will be some people after you, who will be dishonest and will not be trustworthy and will give evidences without being asked to give witness, and will vow but will not fulfill their vows, and fatness will appear among them."

"Whoever amongst you has to praise his brother should say, 'I think that he is so and so, as only ALLAH knows exactly the truth".

"Whoever takes a false oath in order to grab others property, then ALLAH will be angry with him when he will meet Him."

"Establish the prayer, speak the truth, be chaste, keep promises and pay back trusts."

"He, who makes peace between the people by inventing good information or saying good things, is not a liar".

"If somebody innovates something which is not in harmony with the principles of our religion, that thing is rejected."

"From among all the conditions which you have to fulfill, the conditions which make it legal for you to have relations after the marriage contract have the greatest right to be fulfilled."

"Do not offer a high price for a thing which you do not want to buy, in order to deceive the people. No Muslim should offer more for a thing already bought by his Muslim brother, nor should he demand the hand of a girl already engaged to another Muslim."

"It is better for you to leave your inheritors wealthy than to leave them poor, and whatever you spend for ALLAH's sake will be considered as a charitable deed even the handful of food you put in your wife's mouth."

"The laws of inheritance for the male is double the amount inherited by the female, and for each parent a sixth of the whole legacy and for the wife an eighth or a fourth and for the husband a half or a fourth."

"The signs of a hypocrite are three: Whenever he speaks he tells a lie; whenever he is entrusted he proves dishonest; whenever he promises he breaks his promise."

"Fulfill the awes of mother after her death, on her behalf."

"Avoid the seven great destructive sins. To join others in worship along with ALLAH, to practice sorcery, to kill the life which ALLAH has forbidden except for a just cause, to eat up usury, to eat up an orphan's wealth, to give back to the enemy and fleeing from the battlefield at the time of fighting, and to accuse chaste women."

"If one helps a person in matters concerning his riding animal by helping him to ride it or by lifting his luggage on to it, all this will be regarded charity. A good word, and every step one takes to offer the compulsory Congregational prayer, is regarded as charity; and guiding somebody on the road is regarded as charity."

"You gain no victory or livelihood except through the blessings and invocations of the poor amongst you."

"Journey is a piece of torture, for it disturbs one's sleep, eating and drinking. So, when you fulfill your job, you should hurry up to your family."

"Treat the people with ease and don't be hard on them; give them glad tidings and don't fill them with aversion; and love each other, and don't differ."

"The sun and the moon do not eclipse because of someone's death or birth, but they are two signs amongst the Signs of ALLAH. So, if you see them offer Prayers."

"Whoever spends a couple of objects in ALLAH's cause, will be called by the Gatekeepers of Paradise."

"Whoever amongst your followers die without having worshipped others besides ALLAH, will enter Paradise or will not enter the Hell Fire."

"Don't you know that angels do not enter a house wherein there are pictures of living life."

"Wherever the time for the prayer comes upon you, perform the prayer, for all the earth is a place of worshipping for you."

"Do not exaggerate in praising me as the Christians praised the son of Mary, for I am only a Slave. So, call me the Slave of ALLAH and His Apostle."

"When your enemy comes near to you and overcome you by sheer number, shoot at them but use your arrows sparingly."

"A man's spending on his family is a deed of charity."

"Whoever has one of the following four characteristics will have one characteristic of hypocrisy unless and until he gives it up. 1. Whenever he is entrusted, he betrays. 2. Whenever he speaks, he tells a lie. 3. Whenever he makes a covenant, he proves treacherous.

4. Whenever he quarrels, he behaves in a very imprudent, evil and insulting manner."

"Do good deeds which is within your capacity without being overtaxed as ALLAH does not get tired of giving rewards but you will get tired and the best deed in the sight of ALLAH is that which is done regularly."

"Offer prayers perfectly, pay the obligatory charity and be sincere and true to every Muslim."

"When the power or authority comes in the hands of unfit persons, then wait for the Hour (Dooms day)."

"ALLAH does not take away the knowledge, by taking it away from the hearts of the people, but takes it away by the death of the religious learned men till when none of them remains, and people will take as their leaders ignorant persons who when consulted will give their verdict without knowledge. So they will go astray and will lead the people astray."

"The person, who looks after an orphan and provides for him, will be in Paradise and the one who looks after and works for a widow and for a poor person is like a warrior fighting for ALLAH's Cause."

"If any Muslim plants any plant and a human being or an animal eats of it, he will be rewarded as if he had given that much in charity."

"Anybody who believes in ALLAH and the Last Day should not harm his neighbor, entertain his guest generously and talk what is good or keep quiet and abstain from all kinds of evil and dirty talk."

"Save yourselves from the Hell Fire even if with one half of a date fruit given in charity, and if this is not available, and then save yourselves by saying a good pleasant friendly word."

"The best among you are those who have the best manners and character."

"Whoever does not give up false statements by telling lies, and evil deeds, and speaking bad words to others, ALLAH is not in need of his fasting, leaving his food and drink."

"If it is indispensable for anyone of you to praise someone, then he should say, 'I think that he is so-and-so,' if he really thinks that he is such, and no-one can sanctify anybody before ALLAH."

"All the sins of my followers will be forgiven except those who commit a sin openly or disclose their sins to the people."

"The strong is not the one who overcomes the people by his strength, but the strong is the one who controls himself while in anger."

"Make things easy for the people, and do not make it difficult for them, and make them calm with glad tidings and do not repulse them."

"It is not lawful for a guest to stay with his host for such a long period so as to put him in a critical position."

"People reduce the proportion of what they bequeath by will to the One-third, yet even one third is too much."

CHAPTER 13

"**I**t is better for you to keep some of the property for yourself."

"In connection with the guardian of an orphan, that if he is poor he can have for himself from the orphan's wealth what is just and reasonable according to the orphan's share of the inheritance."

"Seek refuge with God from helplessness, laziness, cowardice and feeble old age; also refuge with God from afflictions of life and death and from the punishment in the grave."

"The best JIHAD for women is the performance of HAJJ."

"Good word, and every step one takes to offer the compulsory Congregational prayer, is regarded as charity; and guiding somebody on the road is regarded as charity."

"You gain no victory or livelihood except through the blessings and invocations of the poor amongst you."

"Permission to take part in JIHAD is not preferred over than exerting yourself in parent's service, if they are alive."

"Three persons will get their reward twice. (1) a person who has a slave girl and he educates her properly and teaches her good manners properly and then manumits or marries her. (2) A believer from the people of the scriptures who has been a true believer and then he believes in the Prophet (Mohamed). Such a person will get a double reward. (3) a slave who observes ALLAH's Rights and Obligations and is sincere to his master."

"Free the captives feed the hungry and pay a visit to the sick."

"A time will come when one will not care how one gains one's money, legally or illegally."

"Do not revert to disbelief after me by striking the necks of one another."

"The prescribed Law of ALLAH is the equality in punishment in cases of murders, etc."

"There is no harm for you if you trade, seeking of the Bounty of your Lord during the HAJJ season."

"Keep some of your wealth as it is good for you." "Women are allowed to go out for their needs."

"The best among you are those who learn the Qur'an and teach it."

"A matron should not be given in marriage except after consulting her; and a girl should not be given in marriage except after her permission."

"If anyone of you is invited to a wedding banquet, he must go for it, accept the invitation and visit them."

"Your body has a right over you, your eyes have a right over you and your wife has a right over you."

"If the wife of anyone of you asks permission to go to the mosque, he should not forbid her."

"A woman cannot re-marry the first husband unless the second husband consummates his marriage with her, just as the first husband had done."

"ALLAH has forgiven my followers the evil thoughts that occur to their minds, as long as such thoughts are not put into action or uttered."

"If someone divorces his wife just in his mind, such an unuttered divorce has no effect."

"If you get a thing in possession, remember and recognize its tying material and its container, and make public announcement about it for one year. If somebody comes and identifies it then give it to him, otherwise add it to your property."

"The one who looks after a widow or a poor person is like a warrior, who fights for ALLAH's Cause, or like him who performs prayers all the night and fasts all the day."

'The best alms is that which is given when one is rich, and a giving hand is better than a taking one, and you should start first to support your dependents."

"Do not wear silk and do not drink in silver or golden vessels, and do not eat in plates of such metals, for such things are for the unbelievers in this worldly life and for us in the Hereafter."

"If the 'Isha' prayer is proclaimed and supper is served, take your supper first"

"All drinks that intoxicate are unlawful (to drink)."

"The example of a believer is that of a fresh tender plant; from whatever direction the wind comes, it bends it, but when the wind becomes quiet, it becomes straight again. Similarly, a believer is afflicted with calamities but he remains patient till ALLAH removes his difficulties."

"No Muslim is afflicted with harm because of sickness or some other inconvenience, but that ALLAH will remove his sins for him as a tree sheds its leaves."

"So be moderate in your religious deeds and do the deeds that are within your ability: and none of you should wish for death, for if he is a good doer, he may increase his good deeds, and if he is an evil doer, he may repent to ALLAH."

"ALLAH will not look, on the Day of Resurrection, at a person who drags his gown behind him out of pride and arrogance."

"It is one of the great sins, the forged statement or the false witness."

"He orders us to offer prayers; to give alms; to be chaste; and to keep good relations with our relatives."

"I will keep good relation with the one who will keep good relation with your Kith and Kin."

"Whoever is in charge of the daughters and treats them generously, and then they will act as a shield for him from the Hell Fire."

"A neighbor should not look down upon its neighbors, as anybody who believes in ALLAH and the Last Day should speak good or keep quiet."

"The best among you are those who have best manners and character."

"Abusing a Muslim is an evil-doing, and killing him is disbelief."
"Whoever does not give up false statements i.e. telling lies, and evil deeds, and speaking bad words to others, ALLAH is not in need of his fasting, leaving his food and drink."

"Beware of suspicion, for suspicion is the worst of false tales; and do not look for the others' faults and do not spy, and do not be jealous of one another, and do not desert one another, and do not hate one another."

"The people of Paradise comprise every obscure unimportant humble person, and if he takes ALLAH's Oath that he will do that thing, he will do and about the people of the Hell Fire, they comprise every cruel, violent, proud and conceited person."

"And the better of the two will be the one who greets the other first."

"When you intend going to bed at night, put out the lights, close the doors, tie the mouths of the water skins, and cover your food and drinks."

"Always adopt a middle, moderate, regular course whereby you will reach your target of Paradise."

"If anyone of you looked at a person who was made superior to him in property and in good appearance, then he should also look at the one who is inferior to him, and to whom he has been made superior."

"A Muslim has to listen to and obey the order of his ruler whether he likes it or not, as long as his orders involve not one in disobedience to ALLAH, but if an act of disobedience to ALLAH is imposed one should not listen to it or obey it."

"If you ever take an oath to do something and later on you find that something else is better, then you should expiate your oath and do what is better."

"I am only a human being, and you people come to me with your cases; and it may be that one of you can present his case eloquently in a more convincing way than the other, and I give my verdict according to what I hear. So if ever I judge by error and give the right of a brother to his other then he, the latter should not take it, for I am giving him only a piece of Fire."

"There is no envy if a person whom ALLAH has given wealth and he spends it in the right way, and a person whom ALLAH has given wisdom and he gives his decisions accordingly and teaches it to the others."

ARABIC DEFINITIONS

AHL AL KITAB : People of book
AL AMEEN : Trustworthy
ALHUMDULLILAH : Thank God
ANSAR : Helpers of Medina
ARKAN : Article to faith
ASHRAF UL MAQLUQAAT : Esteemed creed
ASTAGHFIRULLAH : Forgive God
AD ': Tribe of Arabia
AYAAH : QORANIC verses
AZAN : Call to Islamic Prayers
BANI HASHIM : Clan of prophet Mohamed
BIDAH : Advocating unrecorded practise
DUA : Supplication or invocation submitted to God
EID-UL-FITR : Religious festival marking end of RAMADAN
EID-UL-ADHA : Feast of sacrifice performed after HAJJ
EISA ; Reference to Prophet Jesus
EHSAN : Perfection/Excellence
FIDYA : Religious donations
FARAID : Obligatory religious duties
FIQH : Islamic Jurisprudence
FASIQ : Violator of Islamic law
AHADITH : Prophet's Quotations
HIJAB : Veil or covering over body.
HIJRA : Islamic Calendar marking the immigration
HAJAR-AL-ASWAD : Black stone in KABAH
HAJJ : Annual Islamic pilgrimage to Mecca, once in lifetime
HALAL : Permissible object or action.
HANIF : A designated righteous true believer
HARAM : Forbidden
HUDAYBIY YAH : Important historic treaty
HUFFAZ : memorizers of QORAN
IBADAH : Devotion to God (Worship)
IDDAT : Period of waiting after demise of husband
IHRAM : A sacred state of clothing during pilgrimage

IMAM : One who leads the prayers
IMAN : Faith in religion
INSHALLAH : God Willing
I'TIKAF : Practice of praying in solitude
JAHILIY YAH : Pre- Islamic period of ignorance
JAZAKALLAH : Be Rewarded by God
JIHAD : Striving or struggle for a praise worthy cause
JIZYA : Per capita yearly tax
KABAH : Holy shrine of Mecca
KHABEES : Evil doer
KHUTBAH : Formal public preaching in Islam
KHULA : Mutual Divorce
LAILA-TUL-QADAR : Sacred night
MAHR : Obligatory Payment from the groom
MAN O SALWA : Heavenly food send to People
MASHALLAH : Praise be to God
MUNAFIQ : Hypocrite
MOHAJIREEN : Meccan Immigrants to Medina
MUSHRIKIN : People devoting worship other than Allah
NA-KHALAF : Non-dutiful
NASARI : A sect of Islamic Era
NAFIL : Optional Muslim prayer
NIKAH : Marriage in Islam
NIKAH UL MUJTHIMA : Congregation of Marriage
QIBLA : Direction of prayers
QADA : Fulfilling missed duties
QAZI : Judicial Authority among Muslims
QISAS : A form of Islamic punishment
QURAISH : Ancient Meccan tribe
RAMADAN : A sacred month of fasting by Muslims
RABI-AL-AWAL : Lunar month of Islamic Calendar
SAHABA : Associates of Prophet Mohamed
SALAH : Regular Islamic prayer
SALATH UL JANAZAH : Funeral prayers

SALAT UL QASR : Traveler's Prayer
SALAAM : A greeting of peace
SARKASH : Headstrong
SATAN : Devil
SHIRK : Making partners to ALLAH SHARIA : Islamic Law
SHAHADAH : Islamic creed that there is no God but ALLAH
   and Mohamed is the messenger of God
SIYAM : Fasting from dawn to dusk
SURAH : Chapter of QORAN
SUBHANALLAH : Glory be to God
TAQWA : Piety or fear of God
TAWBA : Repentance
TALAQ : Divorce
TAYAMMUM : Dry ablution
TARAWIH : Prayers conducted in RAMADAN after ISHA
   comprising of 8 to 20 units
TAWHID : Indivisible oneness concept of monotheism
TAWAKKUL : Reliance on God
THAMUD : Ancient Civilization in Hejaz
TORAH : God sent words to Prophet Moses
UMMAH : Brethren of faith
UMRAH : Pilgrimage to Mecca at any time other than Hajj
WAJIB : Necessary duty
WUDHU : A practice of ablution or cleansing body before prayers
WITR : Islamic prayer performed in night
ZAKAH : Obligatory charity
ZAMZAM : Spring of water in Masjid-ul-Haram
ZUBUR : God sent word to Prophet David

POST-FACE

With due understanding of the fact that innumerable books are written on this subject by many authors of same belief that may be considered biased by many, as it is expected of Muslims to praise their own religion, so an attempt is made to remain neutral in lieu of the faith and to judge the truth at its face value.

The reference of God is to none other than 'ALLAH' and directives from the book are nothing except from 'QORAN', revealed to Prophet MOHAMED interpreted as per the intelligence quotient of a human mind. The reference of religion is to 'ISLAM' only.

The names of Prophets, Caliphs and people of religious esteem are used with utmost reverence but without the suffixes like PBUH -Peace and mercy be upon him, etc., as this book is also envisioned to be read by believers of other faiths, who may not understand the significance of the same. Only some of the quotations of Prophet called as AHADITH with known authenticity are short listed due to volume limitations.

From the QORAN, certain verses that are oft repeated for due emphasis; stories that explain importance of the revelations; and narrations of coherent issues or events that extend life lessons for all of the mankind, were beyond the scope of this book and have not been completely documented. This book can be taken as an introduction of Islamic literature, which can be separately pursued for details upon reader's interest.

Some Arabic words are retained as-is due to inability of translating them into their full meaning and context but an attempt is made to explain them in simple words given in parenthesis and have been defined further in the appendix placed at the end. The contents are kept simple and logical to be understood by a common man; to be treated as a source of direction for the pursuit of a peaceful life and as a step towards spreading awareness of some social values clarified in pieces.

Many philosophies that contradict Islam, like atheism, have attempted to discover the 'right direction'. However, the right direction was already discovered and defined by Islam. This is in melody with teachings of Christianity and Judaism.

Author

Printed in the United States
By Bookmasters